Prepared by the Worcest<

MW01504341

WORCESTER'S BEST
A GUIDE TO THE CITY'S ARCHITECTURAL HERITAGE

Worcester's Best
Elliott B. Knowlton, Editor

Library of Congress Card Number 84-51697
ISBN 0-914274-12-0

*The activity which is the subject of the publication has been financed in part with Federal funds from the
National Park Service, Department of the Interior through the Massachusetts Historical Commission, Secretary
of State Michael Joseph Connolly, Chairman. However, the contents and opinions do not necessarily reflect the
views or policies of the Department of the Interior, nor does the mention of trade names or commercial products
constitute endorsement or recommendation by the Department of the Interior.*

TABLE OF CONTENTS

PREFACE

The Worcester Heritage Preservation Society (WHPS) was founded in December 1969 by a diverse group of people concerned by the then standard tactic employed by most U.S. practitioners of urban renewal: "destroy the old, build anew."

The goal of this new organization was formally stated: "To preserve for future generations the sites and structures which are significant to the culture, history, and architecture of this (Worcester) area." Its dream was to preserve the best of Worcester's buildings: from factories to commercial structures, from cottages to mansions in order to protect the best of the past and to preserve the city's identity.

In 1966, Congress (by the passage of the National Preservation Act) had authorized the Secretary of the Interior to expand and maintain a national register of historic places. Implementation of the Act rested with the Historical Commissions in each of our 50 states.

The Massachusetts Historical Commission in Boston looked to the Worcester group to help accomplish this work locally. It encouraged WHPS to begin an inventory or survey of Worcester's buildings and neighborhoods. Heritage Society volunteers (amateurs all) working sporadically on this monumental task over the next few years submitted sixteen buildings and districts for listing in the National Register. It soon became evident that the inventory required in a city the size of Worcester was too big a job for volunteers alone.

In February 1977, Brian Pfeiffer, an architectural historian from Cambridge, was hired by the Worcester Heritage Preservation Society to conduct a formal and detailed survey of the city's most significant buildings and districts. The survey was funded by a $5,000 grant from the Massachusetts Historical Commission and a matching grant of the same amount from the George F. and Sybil H. Fuller Foundation. It was supervised by Janet K. McCorison, the Society's Executive Director.

Susan Ceccacci, a member of WHPS and an architectural historian in her own right, became the Society's coordinator and liaison person for the project. The Worcester Historical Museum opened wide its voluminous records through research librarian Dorothy Gleason.

By the end of October 1977, Mr. Pfeiffer and his staff of volunteers had looked at every building along five hundred miles of Worcester streets. Over one thousand buildings were photographed and documented. Of these, 650 were selected by WHPS, evaluated by the Massachusetts Historical Commission, and sent to the Interior Department for final review and listing in the National Register of Historical Places.

This Worcester survey marked the first time an entire city of approximately 25,000 buildings had been analyzed at once and the National Register criteria applied in comprehensive fashion. Judged a great success, this process known as "a multiple resource nomination" is now widely used. Worcester was the first U.S. city to prepare such a nomination. Up to that time sites and buildings were usually nominated one at a time.

The goal of such a survey is to provide architectural and historical background and to offer priorities upon which decisions affecting city planning and historic preservation can be made.

The task of editing the introductory material and building descriptions for this book have been made uncommonly easy by the original authorship of Mr. Pfeiffer. Besides being an extremely competent researcher and keen architectural observer, he has the instincts of a social historian and the facility for pulling together quantities of divergent yet related materials into an understandable and sequential whole.

This editor's job, therefore, has been primarily one of compressing, organizing, and arranging. The most difficult task has been what to leave out. Because we are dealing with a large city, we tried to limit remarks and descriptions to Worcester's best: those structures which through style, architectural excellence, ownership or use, merit the special attention and recognition of National Register designation. For a city of Worcester's architectural, ethnic, and industrial diversity, it is a large and impressive listing. All credit to Mr. Pfeiffer who, with the help of a lot of willing hands, made this survey possible. A masterful undertaking!

Credit should be given and acknowledgement made to others who made this book a reality: WHPS volunteers—Chrysanthi Charalambides, Clara DeMallie, Stephen Jerome, Ellen Kuniholm, Donald Latino, Sandra Lee, Rebecca Moore, Cathy O'Connor, Geraldine Persons, Mary Seaman, and William Seaman; Louise Charbonneau, typist; Dorothy Gleason, research librarian; Harry Allen, Jr., E.B. Luce Co., Adrian Ayson and Ronald White, photography; George I. Alden Trust; George F. and Sybil H. Fuller Foundation; Massachusetts Historical Commission; Worcester Historical Museum; Worcester Bicentennial Commission; WHPS Research and Survey Committee; Bureau of Land Use Control and Office of Planning and Community Development for the City of Worcester. Also the American Antiquarian Society, Harvard Business School, and Worcester Polytechnic Institute. In addition to major volunteer help in the original survey, Mary and William Seaman were responsible for the heroic task of compiling the Index to this book.

Special acknowledgement is due to Janet K. McCorison for her continuous role in the production of this book.

No survey, such as this, is ever complete. Currently, the Heritage Society is preparing a list of additions to the original multiple resource nomination including early twentieth century commercial buildings and structures related to our ethnic heritage.

Elliott B. Knowlton, Editor

Wherever possible, the name or titles of buildings listed appear under their original calling.

Most photo captions appear with a numerical code directly under the building's name or title. This code corresponds to the number on the National Register file folder held by WHPS.

FOREWORD

In March of 1980 the historic and architectural resources of Worcester, Massachusetts were listed in the National Register of Historic Places in Washington, D.C. Register listings for Worcester totalled approximately 650 buildings. For Massachusetts it was the state's first multiple resource nomination— a process which evaluates an entire community rather than nominating buildings individually. As one of the most complete, the Worcester survey was cited by the Secretary of the Interior as an exemplary nomination to be used as a model for the rest of the nation.

During late 1978 and early 1979, the Massachusetts Historical Commission examined Worcester's citywide survey conducted by Brian Pfeiffer, architectural historian from Cambridge, Massachusetts, and a host of local volunteers from the Worcester Heritage Preservation Society. Through this review the major themes and periods in Worcester's history were identified to provide a framework within which to assess individual buildings and districts. This intensive evaluation process resulted in a list of structures which are architecturally significant and which represent all phases of the city's past. Included are civic, institutional, religious, commercial, industrial, and residential buildings.

The rewards were substantial. For the first time, an entire city of approximately 25,000 buildings was analyzed at once, and the National Register criteria applied in a comprehensive fashion. As a result, all structures within defined categories were identified as historic and were listed in the National Register. Also for the first time, preservation concerns could be incorporated into the city planning process, allowing city officials and developers to know at the outset whether or not their actions would affect a National Register property. Further, it is a tremendous aid to the Massachusetts Historical Commission in fulfilling its environmental review responsibilities.

Ever since the Worcester Heritage Preservation Society completed its survey in early 1979, the Society has hoped to publish the results. The Massachusetts Historical Commission is pleased to have been able to provide a grant, matched by the George I. Alden Trust of Worcester, supplemented by the Heritage Society's own funds, to make this book possible.

John W. Curtis
Acting Chairman
Massachusetts Historical Commission

CHAPTER I
NATIONAL LANDMARKS

NATIONAL HISTORIC LANDMARKS

The Historic Sites Act of 1935 authorized the Secretary of the Interior to make a survey of historic sites and buildings to identify those of national significance. Such sites and structures which are found to be eligible for designation as National Historic Landmarks are also recorded in the National Register.

Worcester has two National Historic Landmarks: The American Antiquarian Society, 185 Salisbury Street (1968), and Liberty Farm, 116 Mower Street (1973).

The American Antiquarian Society
185 Salisbury Street
Winslow, Bigelow & Wadsworth

The American Antiquarian Society, at the corner of Park Avenue and Salisbury Street, is a national research library of American history founded in 1812. The age and extent of its collections constitute the basis of the society's national significance, and the reason for its recognition as a National Historic Landmark in 1968. Its holdings through the year 1821 supercede even those of the Library of Congress.

Construction of the Society's present building, its third home, was made possible by a bequest of $200,000 from Stephen Salisbury III, a prominent Worcester businessman and landowner. The society retained two Boston architectural firms—R. Clipton Sturgis and Winslow, Bigelow & Wadsworth—to prepare competing plans for its new building. The Winslow firm's plans were selected, but Sturgis was engaged to supervise construction. Begun in October 1909, the building was completed late in 1910.

The two storey Georgian Revival structure, built of brick with marble trim, rests on a low, granite block foundation. Its octagonal mass, which projects one bay on the northeast (front), southeast, and northwest elevations culminates in a low dome on an octagonal base. A stack wing, roughly square in shape, is attached to the southwest elevation. The marble cornice and frieze which surrounds the building at roof level is repeated on the base of the dome. The Doric portico which covers the main entrance carries a full entablature with triglyphs and a triangular pediment. The doorway itself is flanked by Doric pilasters and repeats the entablature and pediment of the portico on a smaller scale. Windows are 12/12 double-hung sash with keystoned marble lintels. Marble panels with carved garlands are set into the brick between the first and second floor windows on the southeast and northwest elevations.

Alterations to the original portion of the building have been few and minor. In 1924 the marble dome was covered with copper to prevent leakage. Additions made at the rear of the building in 1924 and 1950 repeat the material and detailing of the 1910 structure. A first floor addition was erected in 1972 at the rear of the

northwest side of the building. Though constructed of concrete, it does not detract from the older portions of the building as only its roof projects above ground-level and that has been treated as a lawn terrace.

The American Antiquarian Society is the third oldest historical society in the United States. Only the Massachusetts Historical Society, 1791, and the New York Historical Society, 1804, have a longer history. The American Antiquarian Society was the first to be national rather than regional in its purpose and in the scope of its collections. With holdings numbering close to four million books, pamphlets, broadsides, manuscripts, prints, maps and newspapers, this library preserves the largest single collection of printed source material relating to the history, literature and culture of the first 250 years of what is now the United States.

Isaiah Thomas, founder of the American Antiquarian Society, was born in 1749 to a family so poor that at the age of six he was taken from his mother by the Overseers of the Poor of Boston and apprenticed to a printer. During the genesis of the American Revolution, Thomas's sympathies were with the popular faction. He made his newspaper, *The Massachusetts Spy*, the voice of the Whig party. The paper was distributed from Quebec to Savannah by the couriers of the Committees of Correspondence and, as much as any other one factor, it served to unify the resistance movement in the thirteen colonies. Three nights prior to the Battle of Lexington and Concord, Thomas smuggled his printing press out of Boston and set it up in Worcester. Thomas became the leading printer, editor, publisher and bookseller in the United States after the war. The editions which he published were the best in every field, and were marketed through interlocking partnerships which covered the new nation.

In 1802, Thomas retired and turned his attention to the preservation of the recorded origins and growth of the nation which he had helped to make.

The task of preserving these sources of history for the American people was far more than one man could accomplish. With a group of like-minded men, Isaiah Thomas founded the American Antiquarian Society in 1812. To the newly formed Society he gave the then substantial sum of $20,000 and his library of 8,000 volumes. Worcester was chosen as the site because it was an inland town, safe from the guns of the British fleet.

American Antiquarian Society
88-A-1

Liberty Farm (ca. 1800)
116 Mower Street

"Liberty Farm," the home of Abigail Kelley and Stephen Symonds Foster for almost their entire married life, is located in the hills of western Worcester. The Fosters made it a station on the Underground Railroad, sheltering fugitive slaves on their flight to Canada. Built about 1800, it is a simple Federal-style house of red brick with white painted stone lintels and black shutters. The facade is five bays across, and the rather shallow sides feature gable returns. An attractive distyle Doric portico with full entablature complements the entrance, as do both the fanlight and side lights.

The main portion of the house is completely original and in an excellent state of repair, though there have been additions on the right side and to the rear (c. 1902). With the exception of new doors cut through into the additions, the interior remains unaltered, and the elegant fireplaces are especially noteworthy. Stephen Symonds Foster has been called "a sturdy farmer of his New England fields," and Liberty Farm was reputed to be "one of the best managed and most productive in the district." Indeed, Foster built one of the finest stone fences in New England around his house and barn. Literally every stone in all its 600 feet remains exactly as he set it.

William Lloyd Garrison once told Abby Kelley: "Of all the women who have appeared upon the historic stage, I have always regarded you as peerless—the moral Joan of Arc of the world." Kelley was not only one of the first American women to speak out in public on the issue of slavery, she also defended women's right to a full measure of freedom of expression. "Polite society" was alarmed at such radicalism, and the part that women should play in the anti-slavery movement engendered a bitter controversy. In 1840 Abby Kelley's nomination to a position on the executive committee of the American Anti-Slavery Society precipitated the final split between the conservative and radical camps of abolition. Resigning her post as a teacher at the Lynn (Massachusetts) Friends School, Kelley devoted the rest of her life to reform. She lectured throughout the North on the horrors of slavery and the subjugation of women, risking both her physical safety and reputation.

Liberty Farm
84-A

Abby's husband was a prominent reformer in his own right, a man who vehemently rejected all institutional religion in mid-century America because of its tacit approval of slavery.

The Fosters were also champions of suffrage, and in later years refused to pay the taxes on their farm in retaliation for Abby's denial of the vote. "Liberty Farm," as it was known, was occupied by the Fosters from 1847 until 1881, and the attractive Federal-style farmhouse stands as a memorial to these two radical reformers who—despite opposition—were able to hold steadfast to their vision of a more equitable society. The house was declared a National Historic Landmark in 1973.

CHAPTER II
COMMERCIAL BUILDINGS

COMMERCIAL BUILDINGS

Expansion of the city's central business district was continuous throughout the nineteenth century because of the growth of local industry and population. While much of the demand for more commercial space was met during the mid-century by replacing houses with commercial blocks along Main Street north of the Common, a secondary Main Street business district began to form in the 1860s and 1870s around Federal Plaza Square (then named Franklin Square). Eventually, the central business district extended approximately one block west of Main Street, along side streets, and eastward to Washington Square.

During the 1960s, urban renewal and the construction of Route 290 made major changes in the area's street pattern and resulted in the demolition of virtually all buildings located east of Commercial Street and the Common. During the 1970s, many buildings along the formerly busy Main Street were demolished, leaving many holes in the streetscape. With very few exceptions, the structures remaining in the Central Business District pre-date 1930. The number of buildings in the district (approximately 62) were built prior to 1918. Of these, thirty-three were built before 1890.

photo on page 17
Front Street circa 1900, looking east

1831	Elwood Adams Block	1888	Lamb Block
1851	Worcester County Institution for Savings	1888	Luther-Baker Block
		1890	Lothrop's Opera House
1851	Stevens' Building	1891	Worcester Five Cents Savings Bank
1854	Flagg's Building	1894–97	Second State Mutual Building
1855–57	Mechanics Hall	1895	Central Exchange Building
ca. 1860	Colton's Block	1897–98	Day Building
ca. 1860	Babcock Building	1900	Enterprise Building
1869	Rogers Block	1907	Slater Building
1870	Old State Mutual Building	1909	Union Station
ca. 1872	J. Marcus Rice Block	1912	Bancroft Hotel
1880	Odd Fellows Hall	1914	Park Building
1885	Armsby Building	1914	The Worcester Market
1886–87	Burnside Building	1925	Central Building

Armsby Building
144–148 Main Street
Stephen Earle

Armsby Building
116-CBD-5

The Armsby Building is among the most ornate and well preserved examples of Victorian Gothic design in downtown Worcester. Combining elements of this style with its offshoot, "panel brick" architecture, the building is five storeys high. With a symmetrical facade, the first storey contains an arched entry flanked by one storefront on each side. Although faced with modern materials today, these twentieth-century fronts merely cover the original trim. Upper floors have eight evenly spaced windows at each storey which are trimmed with rock-faced sandstone lintels and sills. Panels of decorative brickwork separate the windows vertically. A slight corbelling supports a paneled parapet at the roof line. At the center of this parapet are a decorative gable and date stone.

Stephen Earle, one of Worcester's most distinguished architects, designed the building which was constructed by C. A. Vaughan in 1885 at a cost of $30,000. As originally planned, the structure contained two storefronts at street level and a boarding house on the upper floors. The block was apparently built as an investment by the estate of George F. Armsby who had been secretary of the Munroe Organ Reed Company in Worcester before his move to Vineyard Haven on Martha's Vineyard in 1879.

Elwood Adams Block
116-CBD-6

Elwood Adams Block
156 Main Street

The Elwood Adams Block, built about 1831, is the oldest commercial block in downtown Worcester. It was built as a two and one half storey building which was enlarged to its present four storey height around 1865. Unchanged from its ca. 1865 remodeling, the block has a facade of six bays width, divided by a central pier into two sections of three bays width. At the first storey are two storefronts (used as a single store) of trabeated granite and iron posts. Windows of the upper floors have rectangular granite lintels and sills. At the roof line is a wooden cornice with modillion brackets. Side walls of the block show faint outlines of the 1831 gable end; however, no change in brickwork is evident on the building's Main Street facade, suggesting that the facade was refaced with pressed brick when enlarged in 1865.

Now containing the Elwood Adams Hardware Store, Worcester's oldest business occupies a site of long standing commercial importance. In 1782, Daniel Waldo, Sr. opened a hardware store on this site for which he built the city's first brick building. Soon after, Waldo's son, Daniel Jr., entered the business, becoming sole owner of the concern in 1791. In 1816, Waldo Jr. took Henry W. Miller as an apprentice. After 1821, Miller and George Rice purchased the business over which Miller gained complete ownership in 1831. Miller, who bought the building from the Waldo heirs in 1865, sold the business in 1886 to Elwood Adams and a partner under whom the store was operated as Smith & Adams. Smith retired in 1891, after which the business assumed its present name.

Old State Mutual Building
240 Main Street

Old State Mutual Building
116-CBD-13

The Old State Mutual Building was constructed in 1870. It is the finest and most elegant integral example of a French Second Empire style commercial building remaining in Worcester, and was the first headquarters for the State Mutual Life Assurance Company. With granite facade, central pavilion, Ionic pilasters, Mansard roof and cresting, this structure is important to the history of the city not only because of the men who were associated with it and with the company for which it was erected, but also because it is unusual in Worcester to find that all three buildings built by a company as old as State Mutual are still in existence.

Incorporated in 1844, State Mutual was the fifth life insurance company established in the United States. Business began on June 1, 1845 with "a guaranteed capital of $100,000" which was "retired" in 1865 after which the company was run as a "purely mutual" concern. The firm's founders and directors were among Worcester's most prominent citizens. From 1845 until his death in 1853, Governor John Davis was its president, followed by Isaac Davis. He was succeeded by Governor Alexander H. Bullock in 1882 who died the same month he assumed the presidency. Industrialist Phillip L. Moen filled out the unexpired term. In 1883 Col. A. G. Bullock was elected to succeed his father and served until 1910.

The company's first location was at 100 Main Street in the rear of the old Central Bank. In 1870 the firm formed a real estate partnership with the Merchants and Farmers Fire Insurance Company to build the block at 240 Main. The two companies shared space in the building from its completion in 1872 until the late 1880s when State Mutual took over the whole structure. By 1894, State Mutual had outgrown its 240 Main headquarters. Construction plans were begun on a much larger building at 340 Main into which the company moved in 1897.

The Old State Mutual Building is now a branch of the Commerce Bank and Trust Company. It is one of many Second Empire style buildings erected along Main Street during the 1860s and 1870s. Demolition of many structures in the downtown area in the mid-twentieth century has left 240 Main one of seven Second Empire style commercial buildings still remaining in Worcester, six of which are on Main Street.

MECHANICS HALL DISTRICT

The Mechanics Hall District contains a group of Victorian Gothic and early twentieth century commercial buildings of exceptionally high architectural quality. Most notable are: Mechanics Hall, a rare Italianate performance hall and commercial block of 1855-1857; Flagg's Building, one of Worcester's last and best Italianate commercial blocks; the Worcester Five Cent Savings Bank, an unusual example of Romanesque Revival architecture; and the (Second) State Mutual Building, Worcester's first "skyscraper" and an ornate example of Renaissance Revival architecture. Other buildings in the district, such as the Day Building, the Central Exchange Building, and the Burnside Building are good examples of late Victorian Commercial architecture, retaining most of the original carved stonework and store fronts. Finally, the Central Building provides a good, unaltered example of late Classical Revival taste. The district's only intrusion is a vacant lot on the south side of Mechanics Hall where a Victorian Gothic style block once stood.

In addition to the high architectural quality of the individual buildings, the Mechanics Hall District is one of the last sections of Main Street to retain the appearance of the dense row construction which once lined Main Street from Lincoln Square to Franklin Square, but which has been fragmented by demolitions over the last twenty years. Finally, the area's densely built character provides an appropriate setting for Mechanics Hall, a building of regional importance which was designed to fit into a commercial district.

Mechanics Hall
321 Main Street
Elbridge Boyden

Mechanics Hall
116-CBD-23

Mechanics Hall was built for the Worcester Mechanics Association, which itself was founded in February, 1842 and incorporated in 1850. A library and a course of lectures were provided for members almost from the inception of the Association. Ground was broken for Mechanics Hall in July, 1855, and the Italian Renaissance building, completed at a cost of approximately $101,000 was dedicated on March 19, 1857. Elbridge Boyden, a prominent Worcester architect, designed the structure. Beginning in 1975, the building was restored, inside and out, at a cost of over $5 million. The firm of Tower and Raymond constructed the building.

Noted for its flawless acoustics, Mechanics Hall housed the most significant concerts held in Worcester. It is the finest hall, as distinct from theatre remaining in the United States from the pre-Civil War decade. Among buildings of its general type and period, only the Philadelphia Academy of Music (a theatre) and Thalin Hall in Wilmington, North Carolina (a smaller example used partially as a city hall) approach Mechanics Hall in architectural excellence. In Massachusetts, only Symphony Hall in Boston, built nearly fifty years later, has, among halls of comparable size, equally fine acoustics.

Stylistically, Mechanics Hall is an outstanding example of the mid-nineteenth century Italian Renaissance Revival. The large-scaled, formal symmetrical facade is built of cast-iron, mastic-covered brick and galvanized iron. Six cast iron piers, faced with rusticated and vermiculated mastic rise through two storeys and support a cast iron belt cornice. These piers divide the first storey into four bays of shop windows. At the second storey level, triple round arched windows fill four interspaces. A radial window with wooden muntins composed of colonettes and rope moldings, is located above the entrance.

At the third storey level, eight Roman Corinthian columns set in pairs and flanked by paired pilasters of the same order support a heavy entablature with a dentilled and modillioned cornice. The four sets of columns and three central bays project slightly to form a pavilion above which rises a pediment. All five bays contain tripartite sash windows surrounded by a fan light—a modification of the

Palladian window.

The most important interior features of the second floor are the two original ticket kiosks, which flank the center of the three entrances to Washburn Hall (at the rear of the second floor lobby), and the handsome broad, balustraded staircases with their fine octagonal newel posts which ascend at each end of the lobby to spacious landings and branch east and west to the third floor. These kiosks are most unusual in form and may be the only remaining examples of their period in the United States.

The Great Hall is on the third floor. This magnificent auditorium measures 80 by 130 feet and is over 41 feet high. A gallery flanks three sides of the Hall and sweeps down along the east wall to the platform stage. It is supported by paired console brackets, richly ornamented with foliate motifs extending nine feet from the walls at the sides. The front of the parapet is decorated by arcaded balusters. A large reception room is located under the west end of the balcony. The east end is occupied by a platform stage. Behind the stage an organ case with paired Corinthian pilasters, ornamental false pipes and a broken pediment of baroque character occupies the central bay. Cloth-backed lattice grillework concealing the organ chamber fill the two flanking bays. In 1864, the pipe organ by Hook was installed.

Above the gallery unfluted Roman Corinthian pilasters divide the walls into bays which contain arched blind openings with deep reveals and enriched moldings. Some of these lunettes were originally glazed. The spaces are hung with oil portraits of Presidents Washington and Lincoln, and various Mechanics Association worthies including architect Elbridge Boyden.

The ceiling is divided into twenty-one panels by beams which spring from the scroll supports. Some of these panels retain the original fresco paintings. The beams are decorated with guilloche pattern panels and paterea at their intersections.

Considered as architectural design, as an example of pre-Civil War Italianate style, as an acoustically superb hall, or as a rare—almost unique—survivor of its 1850s building type, Mechanics Hall is not only a local but a national asset of prime importance.

With the completion of the Municipal Auditorium in 1931, the depression, WWII and the coming of TV, interest in Mechanics Hall began to wane. Wrestling, roller skating, and the Mechanics Association's lecture series barely kept the place alive. Tired and shabby, the old building more than once came close to the auction block and wrecker's ball. But in 1973 architectural historians surveyed the entire structure. Their positive and very affirmative recommendations led to placement in the National Register of Historic Places and complete restoration. Participated in financially by thousands in the Worcester community, work began in 1975. The results have been almost more rebirth than restoration. Once again this handsome building and its magnificent Great Hall glow with elegance, burst with activity, and are full of music.

Flagg's Building
282-294 Main Street

Flagg's Building is by far the best preserved example of an Italianate commercial block left in the downtown area. An extremely popular style at the time of Worcester's great period of growth (mid 1800s), it still retains many of the Italianate details, especially window caps, which have long since been stripped away from comparable buildings. Built just a few years before Mechanics Hall, the Flagg Building is one of the few still standing nearby which gives a feeling of what downtown Worcester looked like as it began to take shape as an important and prosperous industrial center. It was built for Augustus and Elisha Flagg at a cost of $50,000 in 1854 on the site of a bakery owned and operated by Enoch and Elisha Flagg around 1800. The bakery was destroyed by fire in 1815. Use of the site from that time until the rebuilding in 1854 is unknown. An ancestor, Michael Flagg, was one of the original proprietors of Worcester in 1674.

Flagg's Building
116-CBD-23

The Day Building
116-CBD-23

The Day Building
300–310 Main Street
Barker & Nourse

The Day Building was built originally in 1897-98 with a series of additions to the rear along Walnut, Eden, and Sudbury Streets reaching into the first decade of this century. The Main Street facade combines elements of Romanesque and Classical Revival design with carved limestone decoration, cast iron storefronts, and window dividers. The architects were Barker & Norse. Additions built at the rear of the building, which wrapped around the Five Cent Savings Bank onto Walnut Street, have been demolished.

John Day (1851-1907), who gave the building its name, came from Connecticut to Worcester to study law in the office of George Frisbie Hoar. Following his graduation from B.U. Law School in 1876, he practiced here specializing in real estate law and gradually became involved in real estate development. Day bought the land at 300-310 Main shortly after the site at 340 Main had been chosen for the second State Mutual building. At the time of construction, the Day Building was one of the largest in Worcester.

Both the Five Cent Savings Bank and the Day buildings are important to the streetscape as both relate well to the structures around them in their proportions, materials, and design elements.

Central Exchange Building
301–315 Main Street
W. G. Preston (1895-96)
Fuller & Delano (1902)

Built in 1895-1896, the Central Exchange Building occupies the site of the Old Central Exchange Building of 1830, a Federalist style building which was burned in 1843, rebuilt in 1844 and demolished in the 1890s. A five storey structure, faced with limestone, the present building was illustrated in the *American Architect and Building News* in 1896, at which time it consisted of the southern three-quarters of the present facade. Of eclectic Classical design, the facade was originally symmetrical, terminating in end pavillions which rise to broken scroll pediments of pressed copper. At the first storey center is a richly carved limestone entry. Upper floors contain a wealth of carved stone panels, arched window heads set on carved capitals, and other decorated window surrounds. In 1902 the building was extended northward from its original end pavilion. Built in the style of the original structure, this addition has frontages on Main and Exchange Streets, and contains elaborately carved limestone as well as original stone and metal storefronts.

The Central Exchange Building was first owned by Mrs. Lizzie Davis Dewey, daughter of real estate developer Harrison Bliss and wife of Francis H. Dewey. It is probable that Mrs. Dewey held title to the property but did not take an active part in its development. Francis H. Dewey, the son and grandson of prominent local judges, was born in Worcester in 1856, studied law in a local law office and at Harvard University, and in 1879 opened his own law office in Worcester. Mr. Dewey's interest in commercial development was characteristic of many of the city's lawyers who took an active role in the development of Main Street in the 19th century.

Central Exchange Building
116-CBD-23

Worcester Five Cent Savings Bank
316 Main Street
Stephen Earle

The Worcester Five Cent Savings Bank was built in 1891 and designed by Stephen Earle. Romanesque Revival in style, architectural historians call it "one of the most unusual and individual buildings in downtown Worcester." Its rounded corner bay joining the structure's main body by a curved brick wall, and the window trim of bricks with carved ornaments are particularly striking. The use of limestone and buff brick is also unusual and early for Worcester.

The Five Cent Savings Bank was originally incorporated in 1854 by E. B. Stoddard and Rev. Edward Everett Hale, "to attract the attention of the young and induce them to form habits of economy and industry." Business was first conducted from the book store of its first treasurer, Clarendon Harris. Between 1892 and 1903 the Quinsigamond Bank occupied the building's first floor and the Savings Bank

Worcester Five Cent Savings Bank
116-CBD-23

occupied the second. After 1903, the former was liquidated and the latter took occupancy of the first floor. In 1953 the Five Cent Savings Bank expanded to occupy the entire building, and later changed its corporate name to Consumers Savings Bank.

Central Building
322–332 Main Street

Central Building
116-CBD-23

Of classically derived design, the Central Building is a seven storey, steel-frame structure faced with dressed limestone. The building has a symmetrical facade arranged about a central court, facing Walnut Street, although the building's most prominent elevation faces Main Street. The first two storeys of the Main Street elevation contain metal storefronts, embossed with a variety of classical motifs, all in original condition. Upper floors are largely undecorated, except for a decorated stone course (top of second storey), a cast iron frieze, and copper cornice with cresting at the roof line. Among the last major office blocks built downtown before the Great Depression, the Central Building is a well preserved example of its period.

Burnside Building
335–343 Main Street
Bradlee, Winslow & Wetherell

Burnside Building
116-CBD-23

The Burnside Building is a five storey brick block with ornate sandstone trim. Designed as a row building, the structure's Main Street facade originally contained storefronts (first storey) and plate-glass display windows (second storey) set in cast iron surrounds. This original arrangement of the first two storeys is now covered by modern materials. The building's upper three storeys are symmetrically arranged about a narrow center bay. At the roof line is a wide sandstone entablature, above which is a shallow cornice of egg-and-dart moulding and modillions. Although employing elements of Romanesque Revival design, the Burnside Building does not fit purely into a single style.

Among the larger commercial blocks of the 1800s, the Burnside Building was built by the heirs of Samuel Burnside, a local lawyer, on the site of an earlier two storey commercial building. Acting as a corporate body, the Burnside heirs received plans for the building from the Boston firm of Bradlee, Winslow & Wetherell.

Second State Mutual Building
340 Main Street
Peabody & Stearns

Built in 1894–1897 as Worcester's first "skyscraper," the Second State Mutual Building (now known as the Commerce Building) is a nine storey, steel-frame structure, faced with dressed white marble. The building is of extremely ornate, Renaissance Revival design, rising from a one storey base of rusticated piers to an intermediate two storey stage of deeply incised stonework. Upper floors are faced with dressed marble ashlar. The building's Main Street facade is symmetrical with two storefronts on each side of the main entry. Above the entry is a Palladian window framed by pilasters and Corinthian columns, with a deep, coffered frame. At the roof line is a cornice with modillions. Along the Maple Street edge of this property is an eight storey addition, built in the early twentieth century. Built of buff brick with limestone trim, this addition is largely undecorated and is connected to the 1897 building by bridges.

Regarded as "the first modern office building in the city" at the time of its construction, the State Mutual Building was the second office building constructed for the State Mutual Life Assurance Company (the first was at 240 Main Street). Planned as a lavish corporate symbol, it contained a large interior court with a grand staircase and an arcaded loggia at the second storey. The building's top floor was occupied in 1897 by the Commonwealth Club and Brigham's Restaurant, while the storefronts were occupied by various tenants until 1907, after which all were occupied by banks and investment counsellors. Except for the alteration of the main entry and some of the storefronts, the building is intact.

Second State Mutual Building
116-CBD-23

(End of Mechanics Hall District)

Worcester County Institution for Savings
365 Main Street

E. Boyden (1851)
Winslow & Bigelow (1906)

Worcester County Institution for Savings
130-CBD-29

The WCIS building fronting on Main Street and extending along Foster from Main to Norwich Streets, consists of two structures connected in 1969 when an alley running from Foster Street was built over. The earliest section of the building is the rear portion built in 1851 as a joint venture between the old Worcester Bank (parent of the present WCIS) and the Boston and Worcester Railroad Company. Called the Bank Block, this three storey building was illustrated in "The Cottage Builders' Manual" of 1856 as "a fine specimen of its kind."

In its original form the block had recessed, curved corners, broken scroll pediments over the second storey windows, bracketed flat hoods over the third storey windows, a deep cornice with carved brackets, and trabeated granite storefronts. Of the foregoing details only the storefronts and brackets remain. Other ornaments were removed in 1969 when the exterior was stuccoed and incised to resemble the masonry of the front section. An additional detail survives in the projecting bay window added on the Norwich Street side in the early twentieth century. In 1952 the bank purchased the railroad's interest in the building.

In 1906, the Institution for Savings moved to a newly completed building at 365 Main Street, designed by Winslow & Bigelow of Boston, and built by Norcross Brothers. The Main Street building is approximately three storeys high with an open bank hall at its center. The building is faced with dressed granite and the facade is quite symmetrical with monumental Doric columns at its center. Extending around the building's north and west elevations are an entablature with triglyphs, cornice and parapet. Reminiscent of Greek Revival architecture, the Main Street building is unaltered except for some modern sash and a modern entry.

Chartered in 1828, the Worcester County Institution for Savings is the city's first savings bank.

Slater Building
390 Main Street
Frost, Briggs & Chamberlain

Slater Building
130-CBD-32

Constructed by the firm of Norcross Brothers, the Slater Building was in 1907 the city's "second high building or skyscraper . . ." The Slater Building is a steel-frame structure, ten storeys high, rising from a two storey base of rusticated granite piers with an ornately carved entry on its Main Street facade. Storeys three through ten are faced with dressed Indiana limestone. The building's ninth and tenth storeys contain a loggia-like arrangement in their center five bays, each of which is framed by two storey half columns with Corinthian capitals. At the roofline is a dentilled cornice with modillions, above which is a copper cresting.

Upon completion the building had storefronts along its street frontages, an arcade of stores at the second storey, and offices on the top eight floors. Although windows of the first two storeys have been changed, the Slater Building remains substantially intact, one of the city's finest early "skyscrapers." It was erected by the trustees of H. N. Slater, Jr.'s estate. Mr. Slater was a mill owner in Webster.

LOWER PLEASANT STREET DISTRICT CA. 1869-1890

The north side of Pleasant Street, including the corner of Main and Pleasant Streets, contains the city's best remaining cluster of Victorian row buildings, three of which: Lothrop's Opera House, Odd Fellows Hall, and the Rice Block, are architecturally unique.

Prior to 1844, land in this area was owned by Judge Nathaniel Paine who had a house and garden here. In 1844 Paine's son, Charles, built a four storey brick commercial block along the property's Main Street frontage. The younger Paine subdivided the remainder of the lot which was built up with frame houses and a Baptist church. Commercial pressure from the growing business district, beginning in the late 1860s, brought about the elimination of earlier houses and brought the area to its present appearance. The buildings within the district will be discussed in order of location, rather than building date.

Rogers Block
418–426 Main Street
corner of Pleasant and Main

Built in 1869, the Rogers Block is a four storey brick building with a fifth storey set beneath a slate mansard roof. The building occupies a prominent corner lot facing City Hall and has ten bays of equal width facing Main Street and ten bays (of slightly greater width) fronting on Pleasant Street. Original details include dressed granite window caps and sills set on consoles, paired brackets, a dentilled cornice and dormers with arched heads. In the 1890s the building's original four storefronts were expanded to extend along the entire Pleasant Street facade. Above the rebuilt storefronts, plate glass display windows were added. Present storefronts and display windows follow the lines of the 1890s renovation, but have been

Rogers Block
130-CBD-57

covered with modern materials.

The Rogers Block, located at one of Worcester's busiest commercial locations, was built to replace a smaller brick block of 1844. The building's owner, Thomas Rogers (1818–1901) came to Worcester from Holden, Massachusetts in 1840. In 1841 he formed a shoe manufacturing company (Smith & Rogers) which was put out of business by losses from a fire. Having moved briefly to Oswego, New York, Rogers returned to Worcester in 1842 and began manufacturing shoes, remaining in business until 1873 when he retired to manage his extensive real estate holdings throughout the city of Worcester.

Odd Fellows Hall
9–15 Pleasant Street

Built in 1880, the Odd Fellows Hall is an exceptional local example of Victorian Gothic architecture. The only commercial block of its style extant in Worcester, the building is five storeys high with a facade of pressed brick. Dominating the facade is an off-center pavilion which projects slightly and rises above the fourth storey to a steep gable. Facade windows are grouped and have ornate trimmings which rise by storey. Among the building's fine unaltered details are bandings of stone and black brick, original ironwork, stylized carved stonework and a stone name plaque. Alterations to this building are limited to new materials applied over storefronts.

Although known locally as the Odd Fellows Hall, this block was never owned by the organization, but rather was owned jointly by Edwin Morse and Thomas Rogers. The building's upper floors were designed for and rented to the Odd Fellows at the time of the building's completion, while the first storey contained storefronts.

Lothrop's Opera House
17–27 Pleasant Street
Cutting & Forbush

Built in 1890 and designed by Cutting & Forbush, Lothrop's Opera House has an unusual, nearly unornamented facade. The structure is faced with yellow/brown Roman brick and the four storey facade is dominated at its center by two recessed wall panels which terminate at the third storey in low, semi-eliptical lights. Fenestration on either side of, and above these panels, is irregular. It is likely that much of the facade's severity and lack of windows results from the difficulty of fitting a theater onto the building's restricted site.

Lothrop's Opera House was built for Ransom C. Taylor (Worcester's largest real estate developer), and is now the last nineteenth century theater in Worcester. Alterations to its exterior are superficial.

J. Marcus Rice Block
29–35 Pleasant Street

The Rice Block, built ca. 1872–1878, is an ornate Second Empire style building of three full storeys height with a fourth storey beneath the mansard roof. Although the first storey now contains modern storefronts, the second and third storeys retain their original granite facings which bear various carved decorations and recessed panels. Occupying the next-to-last bay at each end of the symmetrical facade are two storey oriels which rise from the top of the first storey and are ornately trimmed with brackets, incised decoration, and applied foliate woodwork. The roof has several types of dormers, all of which retain their original trim.

Divided internally into two structures, the Rice Block may have been built in two sections, the first of which may have been the building's eastern half. In 1872, J. Marcus Rice, a physician, both lived and worked at 29 Pleasant Street. By 1878 the building was completed on its present site; subsequent house directories indicate that Rice continued to live at 29 Pleasant Street while renting 35 Pleasant to a grocer (storefront) and eleven lodgers (upper floors).

Lower Pleasant Street District
130-CBD-57

Lamb Block
39–43 Pleasant Street
E. Boyden & Son

   The Lamb Block was built in 1888 and designed by Elbridge Boyden & Son, architects. Originally five storeys high, the Lamb Block has lost its top two floors. Except for the superficial covering of storefronts with modern signs and panelling, the building's first three floors are unaltered and contain exceptionally fine marble window trim columns, capitals and carved swag panels. Set between courses of marble mouldings, on the second and third stories, are patterned terra cotta tiles. Carved gray marble and terra cotta also trim the building's arched entry. Particularly unusual is the variety of semi-circular and three-sided oriels which dominate the facade.
   Built for the heirs of Russell Lamb, this block originally contained three storefronts and apartments on the upper floors.

Luther Baker Block
45–49 Pleasant Street
Barker & Nourse

   Designed by Barker & Nourse and built in 1888, the Baker Block is a four storey brick building resembling three-deckers of its period (except for its additional storey). The building is trimmed with decorative brick panels, terra cotta tiles, granite window trim, and stone bandings, all of which are more elaborate than the usual finish for buildings of this type. Characteristic of residential patterns in downtown Worcester, the Baker Block had four tenants in 1890, each of whom rented rooms to boarders. In the early twentieth century two one storey storefronts were added to the Baker Block.

(End of Lower Pleasant Street District)

The Bancroft Hotel
130-CBD-59

The Bancroft Hotel
50 Franklin Street
Esenwein & Johnson

The Bancroft, built between 1912 and 1913, was once Worcester's most opulent hotel. Historian Charles Nutt describes it as "one of the most representative institutions of the city originated by the public spirit of a new generation of leaders in city affairs (and) erected by Worcester money and conducted by Worcester men." Named for George Bancroft, noted historian and Secretary of the Navy under President Polk, the building's exterior with its granite, marble, and heavy classical ornament beautifully arranged is among the most impressive in the city. Initial interest in building a luxury hotel began in 1910 when Alfred Aiken, local banker, enlisted the aid of Frank Dudley, president of the United Hotels Company and the Board of Trade. Bancroft Realty Company was formed in 1911. Esenwein & Johnson of Buffalo drew construction plans for a hotel of 225 rooms expandable to 320 rooms. A decision was made to build to the large size. Construction was accomplished by George Blake Long of Chattanooga, Tennessee. Final cost: $1,250,000. The Bancroft was operated as a hotel until 1964 when it was converted to commercial and apartment use. It is now known as "Fifty Franklin Street."

Park Building
507 Main Street
Cross & Cross, D. H. Burnham

The Park Building is an eleven storey, steel-frame structure, covered by a facing of dressed limestone. It was built on land originally owned by Daniel Gookin, one of Worcester's first settlers, whose house on this site burned in 1786. The building's first two storeys are enclosed by a metal and plate-glass storefront (partially altered) which is decorated with a variety of cast classical motifs. The third storey contains evenly spaced windows separated by carved limestone panels and surmounted by a cornice. The fourth through ninth storeys are largely undecorated. At the tenth and eleventh storeys are engaged Tuscan columns, designed to appear as a loggia, above which are a cornice and copper cresting.

The largest of several office blocks built by corporations and holding companies in downtown Worcester in the early twentieth century, the Park Building remained the most prominent element of the city's skyline until the construction of Worcester Center in the late 1960s. Characteristic of the increased importance of corporate activity during the city's last major boom, the Park Building was built for the Park Trust Company, rather than for an individual as had been the case with virtually all commercial buildings prior to 1900. The Park Trust Company was formed in 1915 with a capital of $300,000 which increased to more than $3,000,000 by 1917. In 1927, the Park Trust Company was merged with the Worcester County Trust Company, which, in 1982, became the Shawmut Worcester County Bank. The selection of New York architects Cross & Cross and D. H. Burnham, is also characteristic of the city's large office blocks of 1900–1920, most of which were designed by architects from New York and other cities where skyscraper construction was more widely practiced than in Worcester.

Park Building
130-CBD-38

Enterprise Building
538 Main Street
Fuller & Delano

Steam cleaned, repainted, refurbished inside and out, and returned to its original appearance in 1980, the Enterprise Building is a five storey, brick row commercial/office structure handsomely trimmed with Beaux Arts Classical decoration. Among the best details which set the building apart from most are carved limestone cartouches on the fourth storey, terra cotta window surrounds and swag panels on the fifth, and a deep, pressed metal cornice.

Marked in the 1911 *Atlas of the City of Worcester* as the Enterprise Building, 538 Main Street wears a veil over its origin. Basis for the identification of its architect comes from three sources: a building notice in September 1900 for a brick addition estimated to cost $10,000 to be built for William H. Dexter from the designs of Fuller & Delano; from the increased real estate assessment for a building at the same location from $6,500 in 1900 to $11,500 in 1902; and by the lack of any

Enterprise Building
130-CBD-42

additions or major alterations made to Dexter's neighboring properties (all have the same plans in 1896 and 1911). Based on the foregoing, it appears likely that the use of the word "addition" in the notice is either a mistake or a confused description emanating from Dexter's ownership of the adjacent properties. He was the owner of the Franklin Building (also known as the Dexter Building), and was active in the commercial development of Franklin Square (today's Federal Plaza).

Colton's Block
586–596 Main Street

Colton's Block
130-CBD-45

Colton's Block is a four storey row of brick buildings, containing three vertical units divided by fire walls. The facades of the three units are each four bays wide containing storefronts at the ground floor. The buildings are largely undecorated except for corbelling above the fourth storeys and a wooden cornice supported by paired brackets. Originally Colton's Block contained a fourth unit at its north end, now demolished. Storefronts occupy their original positions, although remodelled with modern materials. The scale, design and details of Colton's Block are characteristic of a number of commercial rows built in Worcester between the 1850s and the early 1870s, although Colton's Block is the only one extant.

It is likely that this row was built for Samuel Colton (1804–1875) who was a co-owner of the *Worcester Spy* until bad health forced his retirement in 1845. After 1845 he "engaged in the plant nursery business at the corner of Main and Austin Streets" and, later, became active in real estate development.

Babcock Building
600 Main Street

A rare local example of granite construction, the Babcock Block's trabeated granite facade is unique in Worcester. The block is five storeys high with elevations facing Main and Austin Streets. Facade windows of the third, fourth and fifth storeys are glazed with double-hung sash, the top halves of which have arched muntins. The block's Austin Street elevation is faced with pressed brick and heavily studded with star-pattern tie-rod plates. Except for its modernized storefront and the replacement of some second storey sash, the Babcock Block is intact. It is likely that the block was built around the same time as the neighboring Colton Block (ca. 1860–1870) for Chester Babcock, a building mover whose house was at 2 Austin Street.

Stevens' Building
22–44 Southbridge Street

The Stevens' Building is one of Worcester's most imposing commercial blocks of the mid-nineteenth century. Built in several sections, the block is a four storey structure with finished elevations facing Southbridge Street and Burnside Court. The building is covered by a low pitched roof except over the center 13 bays of the Southbridge Street facade, where there is a full fifth storey covered by a flat roof. North and south of the central five storey section, the building's walls are divided into bays by brick piers which rise to corbelling. At the roof a deep wooden cornice is supported by paired brackets. Along the Southbridge Street facade are continuous, trabeated storefronts of hammered granite. Other features of the building include granite window sills and lintels, a granite name plaque, and copper cornice over the five storey section of the facade.

The first portions of the present structure were built between 1851 and 1860 for an unknown owner. Containing three storefronts, the original structure is probably contained in the central sections of the present block's Southbridge Street facade. Around 1866–1867 the Stevens Brothers apparently bought the earlier block and extended it northward to Burnside Court where they moved their "sash, door and blind" factory in 1867. By 1870 the two brothers owned the entire block to Myrtle Street, and had built the southernmost seven bays of the present structure as a free-standing block. Between 1870 and 1878 this southern section was connected to the rest of the structure and the building was made to appear substantially as it does today. In 1906 the block was damaged by a major fire, at which time the copper cornice (and perhaps the fifth storey) was added to the central section of the Southbridge Street facade.

The Stevens Brothers were both born in Charlton, Mass. (Daniel, 1818–1888;

Babcock Building
130-CBD-46

Stevens' Building
130-CBD-68

Charles 1829–1885). In 1849 Charles Stevens went to California in search of gold, returning to Worcester in late 1849. In 1850 both brothers went to California and returned to Worcester around 1853, at which time they worked as painters. In 1854 they began manufacturing sash, doors and blinds on Main Street. Later business interests included a flour and grain business which they established in the Stevens' Building and further real estate development along Southbridge Street.

Recently restored, the blizzard of signs which once covered the facade have been removed.

The Worcester Market
130-CBD-50

The Worcester Market
631 Main Street
Oreste Ziroli

The day it opened, the old Worcester Market was believed to be the largest grocery supply store in the United States. Designed by Oreste Ziroli and built in 1914 by J. W. Bishop & Co. (both of Worcester) for the Providence Public Market Co., it prospered and was enlarged during the 1920s. It was sold to Brockleman Bros. in 1929, and to Stop & Shop in the 1950s. Diminishing center-city residential interest precipitated sale again in the mid-'60s to Morgan Memorial. Rectangular in plan, the building remains a unique example of early 20th century architecture with its facing of glazed terra cotta. In addition to designing a number of Worcester residences, Ziroli was the architect of the city's first Christian Science Church at 882 Main Street.

It is one of the earliest prototypes of today's supermarket. The major facade fronts on Main Street. The parapet of this side rises slightly as if to a pediment and contains decorated tile panels proclaiming the name "Worcester Market" in addition to a large medallion bearing a steer's head in high relief. The end pavilions of the facade, and also of the Madison Street side, bear medallions of game birds and rams' heads plus a variety of geometric ornament. Framing of the facade windows and the entry is faced with green, glazed tiles.

The building contained a variety of labor saving innovations. The first floor served as the market, while the second floor and basement were used primarily as warehouse space. Storage was arranged so that goods for different departments were stored directly above or below their respective departments. Connections to them were provided by elevators, thereby protecting customers from having "to watch out for heavily laden trucks hurrying in with fresh supplies."

Customer orders for home delivery were moved to packing rooms by means of carrier belts. The market was laid out with wide aisles running the length and width of the building, and was designed to accommodate as many as 4,500 customers at one time "without noticeable crowding." At the peak of its success, the market handled 25,000 customers "in an ordinary Saturday's trade." In addition to the market hall and warehouses, the building housed a bakery with 20 bakers, a shipping department with 110 workers, a carpenter shop, an electrical shop, and a kitchen to prepare foods for its delicatessen. Vacant for several years, the First American Realty Inc. of Boston bought the building in September 1983. Plans call for renovation and reuse as office space and retail stores.

Union Station
Washington Square
Watson & Huckel

The Union Station was built between 1909 and 1911 to replace an earlier Union Station (now demolished) on the northeast side of Washington Square. The earlier building was opened in 1875. By the early twentieth century, it became necessary to elevate in-town railroad tracks, making the ground level tracks of the 1875 station obsolete and requiring its replacement.

After several years in which proposed plans were altered, the present station was begun in 1909. Designed by Watson & Huckel of Philadelphia, the main body of the station was modeled after a Roman basilica. Construction of the building was delayed by the presence of part of the Blackstone Canal bed (then in use as a sewer) which required special engineering for the support of the foundation. Upon completion in 1911, the Union Station possessed two ornate baroque style towers (each 175' high) rising on either side of the three main entry arches. These towers, faced with white marble, were later removed for reasons of structural weakness. The remainder of the building is set on a granite base and faced with glazed white

Union Station
131-E

terra cotta; the main entries are framed by marble Ionic half-columns. Although much of the building's original ornate exterior remains intact, the station's interior, including the elliptical vault of the main waiting room (80' x 128') with its plasterwork and marble trim, has been largely destroyed.

During its major period of activity, the Union Station served the Boston & Albany, the Boston & Maine, the New York & New Haven and the New York Central Railroad Companies. During the early twentieth century the station was an object of civic pride for its vast scale, elaborate classical design and heavy train traffic. Despite the structure's present neglected state, it retains major elements of its original design and is the city's most imposing example of Beaux Arts Classical architecture, one which also serves as a major local landmark by virtue of its grand scale and prominent site.

CHAPTER III
INSTITUTIONAL BUILDINGS PUBLIC

INSTITUTIONAL BUILDINGS—PUBLIC

Scattered throughout the city's neighborhoods, publicly owned buildings and sites consist primarily of schools and firehouses. The largest number were built before 1900 and most are still in use. In addition, there are a few government buildings, two park sites, a former police station, a state hospital, and a memorial tower. The buildings in this category were selected for their architectural quality, as representative examples of building types, and because of the central role they have played in this community's development.

1854	Elm Park
1898	City Hall and Common
1900	Bancroft Tower
1911	Green Hill Park Shelter
1918	Waldo Street Police Station
1876–1929	Worcester State Hospital

ca. 1845–51	Henry Prentice Cottage
1851	S. B. Watson Cottage
1874–77	Main Hospital
1874–77	Old Laundry
1874–77	Old Boiler Room
1874–77	Stable
prior to 1896	Farm House
ca. 1900–06	Nurses' Home
1906	Attendants' Home
ca. 1920s	21, 22, 23, 24 Hospital Avenue

photo on page 43
City Hall from the Common
130-CBD-37

Worcester City Hall and Common
455 Main Street
Peabody & Stearns

The Worcester City Hall and Common in the center of downtown Worcester comprise five acres of city park area including the City Hall building. The Common encompasses a reflecting pool and attractive landscaping. Rose bushes, shade trees, shrubbery and lawns occupy most of the area. A monument honoring Colonel Timothy Bigelow of Revolutionary War fame, and a monument to the War Dead stand on the property. The Old Burying Ground is also situated in the Common.

The first Worcester building designed expressly for town offices was a Greek Revival structure constructed in 1825 at a cost of $9,017.90. It was greatly expanded in 1841 and altered during the ensuing years. Until Mechanics Hall was built in 1857, the upper chamber of the Town Hall was the largest hall in Worcester. The present City Hall stands on the site of the 1825 structure. The Massachusetts State Legislature passed an act in 1894 authorizing the City of Worcester to borrow $300,000 to build a new City Hall.

Designed by Boston architects Peabody and Stearns, and built in 1898 by the Norcross Company, City Hall stands on the site of the 1825 Greek Revival Town Hall which was demolished to make way for a new City Hall. The bulk of the building is Second Renaissance Revival in style, a phase of architecture inspired by McKim, Mead and White's Boston Public Library, while the tower design is derived from the Tetrecento Palazzo Vecchio in Florence, Italy. The structure is a four storey symmetrical rectangular block constructed of grey Milford granite, 85 feet long, 219 feet wide, with the central tower rising 205 feet above the street. The hip roof and four-sided peak of the tower are covered in red tile. There are two chimneys and four skylights on the east elevation roof. Design elements of the structure are arranged in the manner of a Renaissance urban palazzo.

The imposing facade faces west toward Main Street. It is emphasized at the center where a two storey enclosed entrance portico gives rise to the tower. A heavy carved eagle stands over the central archway and entrance. This archway is flanked by a pair of massive curving Baroque staircases which wind around to both sides of the second floor of the portico. An elaborate central doorway on the

third floor above opens out onto a balcony formed by the flat roof of the portico.

The building originally contained sixty rooms, now many more. It was constructed to be fireproof throughout and is decorated in marble, quartered oak and mahogany. The most impressive interior feature is a grand staircase leading from the ground floor to the third floor. Its stairs are of marble, the balusters are of cast iron in a heavy Baroque design, and the hand rail is of mahogany.

City Hall is significant for its architectural style and prominence in downtown Worcester and as the center of governmental affairs since 1898.

Of the original twenty acres of common land set aside in 1669, five remain with City Hall standing on this original acreage. In the New England tradition, the common land was created as a training ground, burying ground and pasture. Captain James Goodwin, the famed "Captain Gooding" of "Yankee Doodle," is reputed to have been an early drill master there. The Old South Meetinghouse was erected on the southwest corner of the Common in 1719. Isaiah Thomas, publisher of "The Massachusetts Spy," read aloud the Declaration of Independence on July 14, 1776 from the steps of the second meetinghouse built on the site of the Old South. This is said to have been the first public reading of the Declaration in New England.

Railroad tracks from the 1850s which traversed the Common were removed in 1877. The Old Burying Ground was surveyed in 1853, and the stones were buried flat underground. The most recent landtaking occurred in 1973 when construction of the Worcester Center complex required realignment of Salem and Front Streets to the north and east of the Common.

Green Hill Park Shelter
George H. Clemence

Green Hill Park Shelter
79-A

The Green Hill Park Shelter is an open pavilion consisting of sixteen square posts of field stone which support a high hip roof with curved eaves and ridge. Part of the structure's south end contains an enclosed area originally planned as a concession stand. The simplicity of the structure's design, its fine construction and Oriental influences mark it as the most architecturally sophisticated of Worcester's park pavilions, most of which were built in the early twentieth century. George H. Clemence was the architect.

The shelter stands in Green Hill Park, a tract of 500 acres which was given to the city of Worcester in 1906 by the heirs of the Hon. Andrew Green. At the time of the gift the property was laid out as a private estate, containing a Victorian Gothic mansion and other buildings (now demolished) which had been occupied by the Green family since the eighteenth century. Unclear references from the *City Documents* suggest that the city hired the prominent landscape architectural firm of Olmstead Brothers to plan paths, plantings, etc. in order to convert the Green estate into a public park, although individual park structures seem to have been designed by local firms.

Bancroft Tower
Bancroft Hill
Earle & Fisher

A memorial to historian-statesman George Bancroft, Bancroft Tower was erected in 1900 on the hill which bears his name by Stephen Salisbury III. It is a 56 foot, two and one half storey structure built of boulders and cobbles trimmed with rock-faced granite to resemble a miniature feudal castle. Asymmetrical in elevation, the memorial has an open arch at its center flanked by two square towers which rise to observation platforms surrounded by crenellated parapets. Rising out of the top of the western tower is a smaller, circular tower.

Situated at the crest of Bancroft Hill in Salisbury Park, this tower was

Bancroft Tower
38-D

designed by the Worcester architectural firm of Stephen Earle and Clellan Fisher. It was built for about $15,000. During his lifetime, Salisbury retained ownership of the parkland and tower, both of which were given to the city in 1907 under the terms of his will. Bancroft Tower is the last of three stone observation structures built in Worcester parks in the late nineteenth century. The others were: Davis Tower in Lake Park, and Institute Tower in Institute Park—both demolished. Of the three, Bancroft Tower was by far the most elaborate.

A Worcester native and good friend of the Salisbury family, George Bancroft is one of the city's most illustrious sons. Historian, diplomat, ambassador, and cabinet member, he founded the U.S. Naval Academy in 1845 while Secretary of the Navy. An imposing monument erected by the U.S. Government marks his grave in Rural Cemetery, and at the corner of Salisbury Street and Montvale Road a granite boulder points to his birthplace a few yards away.

Elm Park

Edward W. Lincoln

Elm Park consists of two parcels: the original Park bounded by Elm, Russell, Highland and Park Avenue deeded to the city in 1854 by Levi Lincoln and John Hammond; and the 60-acre, 1888 addition to the west called Newton Hill. From the latter, in recent years, 20 acres were cut out for Doherty High School and 8 acres for street widening.

The claim that Elm Park is the first public park in America turns on definitions of first, public (acquired and administered by a municipality), and park (exclusively recreational). A plaque in Elm Park proclaims land acquisition made and completed in 1854. Central Park in New York City counters with land acquisition begun in 1853, though not completed until 1856. But the historic importance of Elm Park is not only an arguable claim to national priority, and a positive one to state priority, but of local importance as a landmark in park development. Edward Winslow Lincoln, commissioner of Shade Trees (1870-1885), and of Parks (1885 to his death in 1895) made Elm Park a model with ponds, walks and bridges mixed with use of native and foreign trees and shrubs. Major

Elm Park
115-A

development under his direction began in 1874. When Newton Hill was added it, too, became a model park, its tree-covered drumlin contrasting with the original low-lying section.

Waldo Street Police Station
Waldo Street
George H. Clemence

Waldo Street Police Station
116-CBD-27

Built in 1918 to replace a police station of the 1880s, the Waldo Street Police Station was designed by George H. Clemence of Worcester to serve as police headquarters for the city and as a courthouse for the Central District Court.

Restored in 1983, the structure retains all the elements of its Renaissance Revival style. Three storeys high, the building rises from a high basement to a flat roof. The north and west elevation, and part of the south elevations, are faced with beautifully made pressed brick which are trimmed with extremely ornate terra cotta. The Station's two entries on the west are nearly identical, each consisting of a rectangular brick frame within which are set two roundels and an arched doorway. These entry arches are also trimmed with terra cotta bearing an interlocking foliate relief into which are cast the words POLICE (north entry) and COURTS (south entry). The basement windows, and those in the first and second storeys, are all set by pairs in rectangular brick surrounds. In the third storey, they consist of paired arched windows set in large, blind arches, each arch bearing a marble roundel. Above the third storey is a deep terra cotta cornice made up of dentils, modillions, bead and reel mouldings, and a band of foliate decoration.

Austere, yet of dignified and symmetrical composition, the massiveness of this handsome building reflects a tradition established by the most important American architects of the period.

The recent restoration of this building has provided attractive, first class space for restaurants, offices and shops.

Worcester State Hospital
92-A-1

Worcester State Hospital
Weston & Rand

Set on 300 acres of land bounded by Belmont and Plantation Streets, the Worcester State Hospital (formerly called the Worcester Asylum) was begun in 1874. Occupying the southeastern slope of Millstone Hill, 255 feet above Lake Quinsigamond, the main hospital building was built between 1874 and 1877 (Weston & Rand, architects). It was enlarged in 1887 and again in 1898.

The main building is a Victorian Gothic style structure built of gneiss rubble trimmed with rock-faced granite and red brick. Intended to house 500 patients, the building has been described as built of "intractable ferrugineous gneiss which is practically impossible to use otherwise than as rubble walling." The window and door openings, therefore, and a few belts and relieving arches are laid in red brick while other ornamental stonework is of granite from Mason, New Hampshire.

The plan of the complex was originally symmetrical. Additions to the rear have altered the plan slightly, but the facade still retains its symmetry. More than 1000 feet long, the facade has a 4½ storey central section (the Administration Building) from which rises the great clock tower. A local landmark for more than a century, it is visible for miles. The tower is trimmed with pointed arches, trefoils, polished columns, and cast iron cresting. The Administration Building has a center entry flanked by four storey bay windows, a porte-cochère set on polished granite columns, and brick window trim. Except for a minor brick addition above the porte-cochère, the building is unaltered.

The wings which flank the Administration Building are 3½ storeys high and recede in three stages. Bearing the same design motifs as the main structure, these wings have projecting bays centered at each stage. These bays rise to high hip roofs and ventilator turrets. Centered on the first three storeys of the bays are brick bay windows. In 1887 pavilions of the wings' original design were extended and nearly free-standing circular pavilions were added to two outer pavilions. Designed by George Dutton Rand of Rand & Taylor, these additions were built in the same style as the original structure and nicely complement its design. Fuller, Delano & Frost (architects) enlarged the kitchen in 1898. The addition of sun porches to some of the pavilions about 1930, and the removal of small portions of roof from the outermost wings are the only other alterations to the wings' facade.

SCHOOLS

Aside from a town meeting house, jail, and courthouse, Worcester's earliest public buildings were schoolhouses, the first of which was built in 1738. In 1765 a second schoolhouse was built, and in 1800 the city was divided into ten school districts each of which received a one-room, wooden frame schoolhouse. Such schoolhouses continued to be the rule until the mid-1840s, when dramatic increases in population density required larger school buildings. At the time of its incorporation as a city in 1848, Worcester contained twenty-six schoolhouses, most of which were of the one-room type. Now the city's oldest school building, the Oxford Street School (1847) was one of the first large brick schools. A constantly increasing population created a steady demand for additional schools, and the new city government began to commission architects to design new "model" school buildings.

By the 1870s, many schoolhouses were designed to be built in stages as population increased. During the 1880s and 1890s new school buildings appear to have been designed in pairs. Although the methods of architectural selection are not made clear in city reports, commissions were spread widely among local architects. Many of the school buildings discussed here are now privately owned and are being renovated and reused in various ways.

For information on Worcester Boys Trade School, see Institutional District, page 79; for information on North High, see page 81.

Bloomingdale School
321 Plantation Street

Built in 1896, the front section of the Bloomingdale schoolhouse is a two and one-half storey brick structure with a slate-covered hip roof. The facade of the

1847	Oxford Street
1850	Ash Street
1863–93	East Worcester Street
1869, 90	Cambridge Street
1879, 99	Grafton Street
1885	Freeland Street
1891	Downing Street
1891	English High
1893	Elizabeth Street
1894	Abbott Street
1894	Dartmouth Street
1894	Upsala Street
1896	Bloomingdale
1898	Millbury Street

Bloomingdale School
105-C

Elizabeth Street School
117-D

building is symmetrical with a center entry set between two semi-octagonal bays. Giving the appearance of small towers these bays have recessed wall panels with arched windows (second storey), modillioned cornices and octagonally-hipped roofs with copper finials. Set between the bays is an entry arch with a keystone inscribed "1896." In 1916, the original four rooms of the schoolhouse were expanded by an addition of four more classrooms which had been part of the original 1896 plan. The addition was built of red brick and sandstone, two storeys high with a flat roof. Although plans and elevations of the building were published in school committee reports, no architect was named. While it is likely that the building was designed by a local firm, no other school buildings are sufficiently similar to the Bloomingdale Schoolhouse to allow attribution.

In 1928, a second schoolhouse was built at the rear of the lot. This second building, built of buff-colored tapestry brick, two storeys high, and Colonial Revival in style, is unrelated to the architectural significance of the original Bloomingdale Schoolhouse. Both buildings have been converted to condominium use.

Elizabeth Street School
Elizabeth Street
George Clemence

Designed in the first year of George Clemence's architectural practice, and built in 1893, the Elizabeth Street School contains an eclectic combination of Renaissance Revival and Romanesque Revival stylistic elements. The building is two storeys high, rising from a basement of mottled yellow brick with upper storeys of red brick. Major decorative features are its square-plan entry towers which flank the southern portion of the structure. Each tower contains an arched entry and roundels at the first storey, tripartite arched windows at the second storey, and, above, a high pyramidal roof. Other decorative elements include arched windows, brick diapering beneath eaves and eyebrow dormers. Unlike most other school buildings of its period, the Elizabeth Street Schoolhouse has had no major additions, perhaps because the surrounding neighborhood (Chandler Hill) was fully developed at the time of the school's construction.

Abbott Street Schoolhouse
36 Abbott Street
William R. Forbush and T. William Patston

Built in 1894 from plans by William R. Forbush of Boston (also of Worcester), the Abbott Street School bears a strong resemblance in plan and detail to the Downing Street School of 1891, also designed by Forbush. The Abbott Street School consists of a rectangular-plan main structure from which projects a central pavilion. At the center of this pavilion is a two storey, semi-circular bay which is flanked by entry arches (first storey) and tripartite windows (second storey). Decorative elements of this central pavilion (arched, rock-faced granite trim and conical slate roof) are derived from Romanesque Revival architecture, while trim of the building's main body is more utilitarian in character. This building was constructed by B. C. Jaques, a local builder, at a cost of $20,000. In 1905-1906 a two storey brick addition was built at the rear of the original building. Of similar design to the main body of the schoolhouse, this addition was designed by J. William Patston of Worcester. The schoolhouse was converted into twelve condominiums in 1984.

Abbott Street Schoolhouse
128-B

Oxford Street School
130-O

Oxford Street School
Oxford and Pleasant Streets
William Brown, Barker & Nourse

Worcester's oldest school building, the Oxford Street School, was designed by William Brown and constructed by Captain Edward Lamb in 1847. This simple, austere three and one half storey, red brick building with brownstone trim is composed of the original building, a bell tower added in 1873, and an addition (designed by Barker & Nourse) in 1880. The original building is ridge-roof Classical Revival in style, unadorned by classical ornament, but its proportions and certain structural elements are of Roman inspiration.

The square Italian Romanesque style belltower of matching brick is related to the rest of the building by the windows on its north side and by the treatment of the corners as pilasters. In 1880, the architects reinforced this relationship by repeating the arches of the belfry openings and the corbelling, which projects just below the tower roof, in the arcades of the enclosed porticoes added on the north and south sides, and in the Palladian windows which were placed at that time in the gable ends.

The school was originally known as the Pleasant Street Girls' Primary School. Boys apparently were educated at the schools located on Summer and Thomas Streets. In 1850, boys were admitted to the school on Pleasant Street and classes extended to the secondary level. In 1878 the name of the school was changed to Oxford Street School. A contemporary addition was built in 1982 when the school became privately owned.

English High School
20 Irving Street
Barker & Nourse

English High School
130-I

Built in 1891-1892 from the designs of Barker & Nourse, the English High School Building is a superb example of Romanesque Revival style architecture. The main body of the building is three and one-half storeys high rising from a base of rock-faced granite to a dormered hip roof. Windows of the third storey and of interior stairwells have arched heads of rock-faced sandstone voussoirs. Dormers are gabled, containing windows with arched transoms and decorative brickwork in the gable. Major entries exist on Irving Street and Chatham Street. The Irving Street entry consists of a sandstone and granite porch with a wide entry arch on squat columns and a sandstone railing with carved corner posts. Slightly simpler in its decoration, the Chatham Street entry is set in a rectangular surround with squat columns, foliate carvings and a keystone with a carved lamp. Above this entry is a shallow projecting window sill with elaborate foliate carvings. At the school's southeast corner is a five and one-half storey tower (130' high) with a high hip roof and cast-iron cresting. The exterior of English High School is unaltered, retaining original oak-panelled doors and low granite walls at the property's boundaries.

Opened in September of 1892, this building served as the English High School (the city's second high school) until 1914, when the English High School was re-organized as the High School of Commerce. At this time the Classical High School which had been located at the corner of Maple and Walnut Streets (in a building designed by Henry Hobson Richardson, now demolished), moved into this building. The new High School of Commerce then occupied the former Classical High School building. After 1966 this building ceased to be used as a high school. It has since been used for school department offices.

East Worcester Street School
12 East Worcester Street
E. Boyden & Son

East Worcester Street School
131-G

East Worcester Street is a three storey brick building, built in three sections between 1863 and 1893. The building's earliest portion was built in 1863 on the site of the Pine Meadow Burial Ground (from which the last graves were removed in 1876). The structure was known as the East Worcester Grammar School until 1893 when it was sold to the Norcross Brothers. The schoolhouse, designed by Elbridge Boyden & Son and built by H. W. Eddy and Moses Taft at a cost of $11,706.25, was apparently modelled after the Salem Street Schoolhouse (now demolished) which was then considered to be the best school building in the city. In its present form the former East Worcester Schoolhouse has a rectangular floor plan, paired entries on its north and south elevations, rock-faced granite window trim and a hip-on-hip roof.

Around 1880-1881, the Norcross Brothers, nationally famous builders known for their work with Henry Hobson Richardson, bought land adjoining the East Worcester Schoolhouse and built a planing mill. By 1893 the Norcross Brothers had bought the schoolhouse from the city, converted it to offices and built extensive additions connecting the schoolhouse and planing mill. These additions and planing mill are built of common brick, three storeys high with flat roofs, corbelled cornices and rock-faced sandstone trim. It was in this factory that the Norcrosses "made their own doors, window-sash and finishing . . . doing the same in such an economical manner that they became the despair of other firms doing the same line of work." The firm was incorporated in 1902 and remained in business at this location until 1918.

Although somewhat altered and currently defaced with many signs, this building has been included because of the importance of Elbridge Boyden and the Norcross Brothers.

Downing Street School
92 Downing Street
William R. Forbush

Downing Street School
140-D

Built in 1891, and designed by William R. Forbush, the Downing Street Schoolhouse is an unusual example of Romanesque Revival style architecture. The building consists of a rectangular plan main body, with a projecting central section. Centered on this section is a semi-circular, tower-like bay which contains the stairhall. Flanking this bay are two arched entries surmounted by tripartite arched windows. Additional details include eyebrow dormers on the roof's southside and trim of yellow brick. The building was constructed by W. F. Dearborn at a cost around $35,000. Little is known of William Forbush, who is listed as an architect in the 1886 directory only. Later building notices imply that Forbush carried on an architectural practice in Boston.

Ash Street School
Ash and Green Streets
Elbridge Boyden

Ash Street School
143-D

Now used as a warehouse, the Ash Street School is the second oldest school building in Worcester. Designed by Elbridge Boyden and built in 1850, it was one of nine new schoolhouses built by the city in the wave of civic pride and expansion which followed Worcester's incorporation as a city in 1848. Of the nine, only the Ash Street and the Oxford Street Schools remain.

The Ash Street Schoolhouse is a three storey brick building with a square floor plan and low hip roof. Each elevation is divided into four equal bays by piers which rise to corbelling at the head of each bay. On the north and south sides, separate entries for girls and boys occupy the center two bays of the ground floor. Above these, on the south elevation, is an original fire escape. The building has a deep cornice supported by paired brackets. Except for the removal of its original cupola, this schoolhouse is unaltered. Most of the residential quarter which the school served has been demolished leaving the schoolhouse a rare survivor of the area's development during the 1840s-1860s.

Grafton Street School
144-A

Grafton Street School
311 Grafton Street
Elbridge Boyden and J. William Patston

Located near major Victorian industrial districts, the area around the Grafton Street Schoolhouses underwent nearly constant development in the nineteenth and early twentieth centuries, gradually changing from a suburban neighborhood to an area of dense "three-decker" construction. Corresponding to this increased population density, the Grafton Street School underwent two major additions in 1890 and 1899. Built in 1879 from plans by Elbridge Boyden, this building was designed to contain four school rooms and to replace an earlier, wooden school. Resembling the Winslow Street Schoolhouse (demolished), the 1879 section is a two and one-half storey brick structure of Victorian Gothic design, one of the few school buildings of its type extant. Decoration of this section consists of black brick banding, low window arches with sandstone springers and brick corbelling. In 1890 the northern half of Schoolhouse #1 was added, designed by Elbridge Boyden in the same style as the original structure.

Development of the schoolhouse property was completed in 1899 when a second schoolhouse was built from plans by J. William Patston. A free-standing structure, it is of brick construction, four storeys high with a flat roof. The building's symmetrical facade is trimmed by brick quoining and has a projecting pavilion at its center. The entry consists of brick pilasters and sandstone columns supporting an entablature and cornice. At present both schoolhouses remain substantially intact from the turn of the century.

Dartmouth Street School
13 Dartmouth Street
George Clemence

Virtually identical to the central portion of the Elizabeth Street Schoolhouse of 1893, which was designed by the same architect (George Clemence), the Dartmouth Street Schoolhouse contains two sections. The building's first section, built in 1894, contains an entry tower with an arched entry, roundels, tripartite arched windows and a high pyramidal roof. Attached to the tower is the main body of the building with high arched window surrounds, brick diapering, a slate-covered hip roof and eyebrow dormers. Built in an area that underwent extensive development with three-decker apartment houses in the early twentieth century, the Dartmouth Street Schoolhouse was expanded eastward in 1908. This two storey addition bears some of the same decorative motifs as the original building (arched window surrounds and brick diapering) although it is enclosed by a flat roof surrounded by a stepped parapet. Presently in use as a schoolhouse, the Dartmouth Street Schoolhouse has been unaltered since 1908.

Dartmouth Street School
144-D

Freeland Street School
12 Freeland Street
Barker & Nourse

The Freeland Street Schoolhouse built in 1885 is a two and one-half storey brick building of basically rectangular plan. Projecting from positions slightly off-center on the building's south and north elevations are pavilions which rise to pedimented gables which contain the school's entries and stairways. The major elevation is assymetrical with grouped windows providing light to classrooms at both storeys east and west of the entry pavilion. Major decorative elements of the design are its sandstone water table and window trim, courses of decorative brickwork and panels of terra cotta tiles. The building is enclosed by a hip roof with hip-roofed dormers.

Built during a period of rapid population growth, the Freeland Street Schoolhouse is one of several grammar schools constructed in the vicinity of Main Street south during the 1880s and 1890s, the area's major period of development. The building was designed by the local firm of Barker & Nourse and constructed by Jeremiah Murphy at a cost of $11,444.

Freeland Street School
164-H

Cambridge Street Schoolhouse #1
165-E

Cambridge Street Schoolhouse #2
165-E

Cambridge Street Schoolhouse
510 Cambridge Street
Elbridge Boyden

Built in three sections, the Cambridge Street Schoolhouse contains Worcester's only Second Empire style schoolhouse to have escaped major alteration. Built in 1869 from plans by Elbridge Boyden, the building's front section is a two storey brick structure with a third storey beneath a slate-covered mansard roof. The facade is symmetrical with slightly projecting center and end pavilions, an original entry porch, and decorative brickwork at the cornice. This arrangement of the facade is similar to that of large school buildings designed by Boyden, notably the Washburn Shops at Worcester Polytechnic Institute and the 1867 renovation of Fenwick Hall at Holy Cross College.

In 1890, a second free-standing schoolhouse was built at the rear of the lot. This building is a two and one-half storey brick structure with a square floor plan and hip roof. Trimmed with brown sandstone, most features of this structure are derived from Romanesque Revival architecture, but are without specifically Romanesque decoration. In 1916, a three storey brick and tile Gothic style addition was added to the rear wall of the 1869 schoolhouse.

The Cambridge Street Schoolhouse was built to serve South Worcester, an area which had been sparsely populated until the mid-1850s, when Southbridge Street was extended, providing a direct link with downtown Worcester. During the 1860s and 1870s, the development of industry along Southbridge Street and along the Norwich and Worcester and Western Railroad brought increased residential development to the area. The success of carpet manufacturing in the area, particularly after the mid-1880s, resulted in further increases in population, which, in turn, created the need for additions to the Cambridge Street Schoolhouse. The school remained in use until 1976. In 1978 the city sold the property and the school buildings were rehabilitated as apartments.

Millbury Street School
South Ward Street
J. William Patston

Designed by J. W. Patston and built at a cost of approximately $13,000 in 1898-1899, the Millbury Street Schoolhouse #4 is a two and one-half storey structure, built of red brick and rising from a rock-faced granite basement to a slate-covered hip roof. The building's symmetrical facade is dominated by a gabled central pavilion with two arched entries. Trim of the building consists of a rock-faced sandstone water table, sandstone sills and carved sandstone springer blocks at the entries. At present, the building is unaltered.

Built shortly after the Woodland Street School (1897, now altered) to which it was identical, the Millbury Street Schoolhouse #4 is the best example of a group of similar schoolhouses built throughout the city. The Millbury Street Schoolhouse #4 is the last of four school buildings built on its lot between the early 1880s and 1899, a period during which the surrounding neighborhoods became densely developed with three-deckers. Highway construction and subsequent decreases in neighborhood population led to the demolition of the first three schoolhouses, leaving only the present structure.

Millbury Street School
166-D

Upsala Street School
36 Upsala Street
George Clemence

Built to accommodate the residential development of Union Hill in the late 1890s and early twentieth century, the Upsala Street School was built in three stages, the first of which contains the school's present facade. This original section is two and one-half storeys high of brick construction with a slate-covered hip roof. The facade is symmetrical about a projecting central pavilion which contains a deep entry arch flanked by equal-sized blind arches and roundels bearing the building's construction date—1894. The architect was George Clemence. Above the entry is a shallow balcony with a sandstone name plaque. The building's trim

Upsala Street School
179-A

consists largely of sandstone which forms window sills, lintels and a continuous decorative band beneath the modillioned cornice. Dormers have hip roofs and the building's chimney stacks are panelled.

In 1902, a rear wing was added to the original structure. Of identical design to the original building, this addition seems likely to have been included in the building's original design in order to allow for expansion as the surrounding neighborhood grew.

In 1923, the second addition was built. Attached to the rear wall of the 1902 addition, the 1923 addition is built of brick with sandstone trim. Except for its flat roof, this second addition resembles the design of the earlier sections.

FIREHOUSES

Following the disastrous fires which destroyed large sections of Boston and Chicago, the city government began to build firehouses, beginning with three in 1873, of which only the Pleasant Street Firehouse remains intact. As with public school buildings, firehouse commissions seem to have been widely distributed among local architects. Although the building type is more restricted in plan by function requirements of garage space on the first storey, living quarters and hose drying bell tower, firehouses were built in a variety of styles ranging from the Queen Anne of Fuller & Delano to Renaissance Revival designs by George H. Clemence, and more eclectic combinations of elements of several Victorian styles.

1873	Pleasant Street
1886	Woodland Street
1886	Cambridge Street
1891	Quinsigamond
1893	Webster Street
1894	Bloomingdale Street
1900	Providence Street
1901	Beacon Street

Bloomingdale Firehouse
676 Franklin Street
George H. Clemence

As Worcester's population grew in the last two decades of the 19th century from 58,291 (1880) to 118,421 (1900), the city constructed many new firehouses to protect newly developed residential areas. The Bloomingdale Firehouse, one of several designed by George H. Clemence, was constructed on land donated by William Putnam by W. F. Dearborn and Sons, contractors, at a cost of $12,137.96. The firehouse is a two and one-half storey mottled buff brick structure with a high slate-covered hip roof. On the building's south side is a square-plan tower which rises to an open belfry and high hip-turret. The two engine doors are framed by low arches with limestone keystones. Above are two sets of tripartite windows set in limestone surrounds. Presently, the firehouse is unaltered and is, visually, an important part of its neighborhood.

Bloomingdale Firehouse
119-C

Pleasant Street Firehouse
129-C

Pleasant Street Firehouse
408 Pleasant Street

Begun in 1873 and completed in 1874, the Pleasant Street Firehouse is one of the oldest fire stations in Worcester. The building was one of three which were begun in 1873. The other two buildings were located on John Street (now demolished) and Lamartine Street (severely altered, now used as a police station). Considering the date of its construction and the sophistication of Worcester architects (who were then designing buildings in the Victorian Gothic and Second Empire styles), the Pleasant Street Firehouse appears curiously out-dated for its era. The building's pedimented facade (originally with two arched entries), slightly projecting side pavilion with a pediment and circular light and the open cupola centered on the building's roof are reminiscent of Federalist and Greek Revival style public buildings of the first half of the nineteenth century rather than the more "picturesque" Second Empire and Victorian Gothic public buildings which were being built in Worcester during the 1870s. More in keeping with the period of the building's construction are its window lintels and recessed wall panels with corbelled cornices.

In 1873 the city purchased the Pleasant Street lot from Daniel Waldo Lincoln for $460.60. Although city documents offer an accounting of the building's cost, no architect is named. The building is now privately owned.

Woodland Street Firehouse
36 Woodland Street
Fuller & Delano

The Woodland Street Firehouse is a two storey brick structure built in 1886 from the designs of Fuller & Delano. The building has a rectangular floor plan and a square tower at its southwest corner. At its facade the firehouse rises from a base of rock-faced granite laid in a broken course. Centered at ground level is an arched entry containing the original doors above which are tripartite windows, and a gable with sandstone coping and finial. The building is enclosed by a slate-covered hip roof. The tower rises almost four storeys to a belfry framed by paired arches enclosed by a high hip roof.

The Woodland Street Station is one of Worcester's finest Victorian firehouses, both for its unaltered condition and high quality original design which combines elements of Queen Anne and Romanesque Revival styles.

Almost a twin to the Cambridge Street Firehouse (also designed by Fuller & Delano in 1886), the Woodland Street Firehouse was built to serve the surrounding residential area which grew dramatically in the 1880s and 1890s as existing large lots and estates were subdivided for suburban development. This building is presently in private hands.

Beacon Street Firehouse
108 Beacon Street
George H. Clemence

Built in 1901-1902, the former Beacon Street Firehouse is a two storey brick structure of rectangular plan. The building's facade contains three low-arched bays at the first storey, each of which is trimmed with alternating brick and limestone voussoirs. At the second storey each bay has paired arched windows set beneath a semi-circular blind arch trimmed with brick and limestone voussoirs. Above the arches is a continuous limestone moulding surmounted by marble roundels. At the roofline is a copper cornice with dentils and modillions. At the structure's southeast corner is a three storey tower.

The Beacon Street Firehouse was built for the city's Engine Company #3, which had been formed in 1835. Although the company provided fire protection for the neighboring Main Street south residential area, it is likely that its major purpose was to provide protection for the extensive industrial area immediately east of the firehouse, including the Junction Shop. The building was constructed at a cost of $25,600 by Eli Belisle, a French-Canadian immigrant who was one of Worcester's leading builders. Included in the construction budget was $925.00 paid to George H. Clemence for plans and specifications. Currently privately owned, it is used as a warehouse.

Woodland Street Firehouse
143-LL

Beacon Street Firehouse
142-M

Providence Street Firehouse
155-H

Providence Street Firehouse
100 Providence Street
Earle & Fisher

Designed by Earle & Fisher, and built in 1899-1900, the Providence Street Firehouse is a two and one-half storey brick building with a rectangular floor plan and square-plan tower on its north wall. Although its scale and plan are similar to other firehouses of the period, the Providence Street Firehouse is unusual for its heavy, Beaux Arts, classical trim, particularly its entry set in an eared architrave with rosettes and a pediment. Second storey windows retain original sash and are set in heavy sandstone architraves. Recently restored, the Providence Street Firehouse is in excellent condition.

Built to serve the residential area with which Union Hill was developed in the late nineteenth and early twentieth centuries, the Providence Street Firehouse was designed for the city's Hose Company #8 which had been formed around 1876.

Webster Street Firehouse
40 Webster Street
E. Boyden & Son

Built in 1893, the Webster Street Firehouse possesses a variety of fanciful and eclectic ornament. Characteristic of firehouses of its period, the building has paired entries for fire engines, a one storey wing which leads to the stairway and a tower which rises to an open belfry. Faced with yellow brick and yellow terra cotta, the facade contains the central date panel flanked by brick pilasters with stylized foliate capitals (second storey) and a high arched window surmounted by a decorative tower with an iron cresting. Although some of the building's terra cotta tiles bear classical motifs characteristic of the 1890s, other stylized elements of the facade (particularly its cresting, capitals and hexagonal slatework) are holdovers from Victorian Gothic design. At present, the Webster Street Firehouse is unaltered.

The Webster Street Firehouse was designed by the prominent local firm of

Webster Street Firehouse
163-E

Elbridge Boyden & Son and was built by Eli Belisle at a cost of $16,000. Still in service as a fire station, the building was constructed to house Steamer Company #5 and, later, Hook and Ladder Company #4, both of which served the surrounding industrial and residential district which was known locally as New Worcester.

Cambridge Street Firehouse
526-534 Cambridge Street
Fuller & Delano

Cambridge Street Firehouse
166-A

The Cambridge Street Firehouse is a two storey brick building with a three storey tower at its southeast corner and a one storey wing at its northeast corner. The main body of the building is rectangular in plan with a slate-covered hip roof. The facade rises from a base of rock-faced granite laid in a broken course and contains a rectangular opening framing the two pairs of doors which provide entrance for the engines. Above these doors is a tripartite window with arched transoms. Centered at the facade's roof line is a decorative gable with sandstone coping with finials. Side walls of the building are largely undecorated, except for the rear tower which rises to paired arched windows, a projecting brick cornice, paired arched openings with vents and a high hip roof. With the exception of some modern re-painting, the Cambridge Street Firehouse is unaltered.

Nearly identical to the Woodland Street Firehouse which was also designed by Fuller & Delano in 1886, the Cambridge Street Firehouse was built to serve South Worcester, an area which experienced rapid industrial and residential growth during the 1880s and 1890s, much of which was brought about by the expansion of the Whittall Carpet Mills.

Quinsigamond Firehouse
192-B

Quinsigamond Firehouse
837 Millbury Street
Patston & Lincoln

      Built in 1891-1892 from the designs of J. W. Patston and C. H. Lincoln, the Quinsigamond Firehouse with its high hip roof, central gable and central grouping of three windows is somewhat reminiscent of the Woodland Street and Cambridge Street Firehouses of 1886. However, unlike those two earlier firehouses, the Quinsigamond Firehouse is of two and one-half storey (instead of two storey) height and has a Palladian window in its central gable. Decorative trim consists principally of rock-faced sandstone and a small, carved sandstone cap at the gable's peak. Originally this firehouse was to have been built on Quinsigamond Avenue. However difficulties were encountered in buying a lot with the result that the present Millbury Street site was chosen after several postponements of construction. The firehouse was built by local builder O. C. Ward at a cost of $7,112. It is one of several public buildings along Millbury Street at Quinsigamond Village which give the area the appearance of a small town center, reflecting Quinsigamond Village's standing as a distinct area within Worcester.

WORCESTER'S FIRST BRANCH LIBRARIES

In 1859 the city of Worcester opened its first public library on Elm Street (now demolished). Most of the books in the original collection came from three sources: the former Worcester Lyceum, the Young Men's Library Association, and a gift of 7,000 volumes from Dr. John Green. As the city grew, delivery points were established in various parts of the city. By 1908 the city's expansion to sections distant from the downtown area resulted in a movement to build branch libraries. Around 1912 the city was given $75,000 by Andrew Carnegie to allow the construction of three library buildings: Greendale, Quinsigamond, and the South Worcester Branch. In each case land was donated by industries located in the area.

It is unclear how architects were selected, perhaps a competition was held. The strong similarities of plan and scale among the buildings, however, suggest that much of the design had been predetermined either by the city or by Carnegie. Cornerstones for the three buildings were laid on March 17, 1913.

Greendale Branch Library
Lucius Briggs (Frost, Briggs and Chamberlain)

Designed by Lucius Briggs while he was a member of the firm of Frost, Briggs and Chamberlain, the Greendale Branch Library is a one storey brick structure set on a high basement enclosed by a tile roof. Bearing elements of Spanish Mission style architecture, the symmetrical facade is dominated by a projecting central pavilion. Centered on the pavilion is a carved stone doorway framed by Corinthian pilasters surmounted by consoles and a semi-circular pediment. Elsewhere the building is decorated by geometric brickwork and limestone trim. A plaque on the exterior records the donors of the site as "the Manufacturers of Greendale," including the Allen-Higgins Wall Paper Company, Norton Company, Osgood

Greendale Branch Library
33-A

Bradley Car Company, Morgan Spring Company, Young Brothers, and Worcester Pressed Steel Company.

South Worcester Branch Library
Henry D. Whitfield

The South Worcester Branch Library designed by Henry D. Whitfield, is a one storey, yellow brick building set on a high basement. The facade is symmetrical about a projecting center pavilion. The entry is approached by two flights of granite steps with solid limestone railings. All exterior trim is made of dressed limestone and is derived from a variety of Classical Renaissance sources. Among many fine details are earred window frames with moulded caps, Tuscan columns at the entry, carved stone panels and a stepped parapet. Along the property's Southbridge Street frontage is a low granite curbing. As with the other two libraries built with the Carnegie donation, the South Worcester Branch Library was erected on land donated by local industrialists, in this case: Alfred Thomas and Matthew J. Whittall whose carpet factories were nearby.

Quinsigamond Branch Library
Fuller & Delano

Located at the center of Quinsigamond Village, the Quinsigamond Branch Library is one of several public buildings which give the surrounding area the appearance of a small town center. Designed by Fuller & Delano Company, the building exhibits elements of the Beaux Arts Classical style. It is one storey high, built of brick with limestone trim. The library's symmetrical facade is dominated by a projecting central pavilion which contains an Ionic entry. Flanking the pavilion are tripartite windows set in stone surrounds. The building is enclosed by a flat roof which is concealed by a brick parapet with limestone coping. Land for the Quinsigamond Branch Library was donated by the American Steel and Wire Company which had been responsible for much of the development of the Quinsigamond Village.

South Worcester Branch Library
165-A

Quinsigamond Branch Library
192-A

CHAPTER IV
INSTITUTIONAL DISTRICT

INSTITUTIONAL DISTRICT
Lincoln Square, Wheaton Square
Salisbury and Tuckerman Street Addresses

photo on page 71
Wheaton Square

Lincoln and Wheaton Squares occupy a location which has been important in the city's development since the seventeenth century when mills were established north of Lincoln Square and a wooden fort was maintained in roughly the same area. Although no buildings in the area pre-date 1843, influences of the eighteenth century remain in the site of the Worcester County Courthouse, part of which was donated to the county by Judge William Jennison in 1732 as an incentive to place the courthouse in Worcester. More widespread in its effects was the purchase of land north and west of Lincoln Square around 1770 by Stephen Salisbury I. Salisbury's mercantile success and subsequent purchases of land in the area (a course followed by his son, Stephen II) gave the family ownership of virtually all of the property around Wheaton Square (formerly Armory Square). Beginning with the 1884 sale of the land to the Central Church, Stephen Salisbury III brought about many of the area's buildings by sale and by donation of land and money to the Worcester Historical Society (1890), the Worcester Art Museum (1897-1899), and Worcester Woman's Club (1902). It is also likely that Salisbury III provided the lots for the Worcester Armory (1889) and for the first portion of the North High School (1889). In the twentieth century, the estate of Stephen Salisbury III, which passed to the Worcester Art Museum, made land available for additional institutions by providing sites for the Worcester Boys Club (1928), the Worcester War Memorial (1935) and the Worcester War Memorial Auditorium (1931) which stands on the site of Salisbury's orchard. Although development of the area never seems to have been planned, the early presence in this district of the County Courthouse and, later, the American Antiquarian Society (demolished) seems to have influenced

Stephen Salisbury III, under whose guidance much of the district took form.

At present, Lincoln and Wheaton Squares contain Worcester's greatest concentration of public buildings, one which contains major local examples of Romanesque Revival, Greek Revival, Classical Revival and Georgian Revival styles of architecture.

Worcester County Courthouse
2 Main Street

Ammi B. Young (1843)
Stephen Earle (1878)
Andrews, Jaques & Rantoul (1898)
Stuart W. Briggs and Cornelius W. Buckley (1954)

Worcester County Courthouse
102-W

Built originally in 1843-1845, the Worcester County Courthouse is a large granite structure of predominantly Greek Revival design. It occupies a site which has served as the seat of Worcester County government since the county's formation in 1731-1733. The present facade is symmetrical, containing a central entry recessed behind four columns and flanked by pedimented end pavilions, each of which contains two columns. The southern pavilion of the facade contains the building's earliest section (1843-1845) which was built at a cost of $100,000 by Horatio Tower (carpenter) and David Woodward (mason). Prior to the 1898-1899 extension of the facade, this original Greek Revival style section had a temple front supported by six columns with combined acanthus and papyrus capitals. These columns remain and were distributed across the facade in 1898-1899. The south elevation of the original structure is unaltered, consisting of evenly spaced bays divided by pilasters which rise to caps of tongue and dart mouldings.

In 1878, a small addition of curiously combined Greek Revival and mid-Victorian design was added to the southwest corner of the 1843-1845 Courthouse. Planned to appear as a separate building but of style and color to harmonize with the original Courthouse, this wing is rectangular in plan with rock-faced granite piers which rise to pilasters, which, in turn, support a cornice with a frieze of stylized triglyphs. Above the cornice, at the facade, is a low pediment and date stone. Except for the replacement of its front doors, this section is unaltered.

Continued growth of the county required major expansion of the Courthouse in 1898-1899. A design competition was held in 1897 wherein one of the competition's terms was that the existing granite columns be kept. Andrews, Jaques & Rantoul of Boston won the commission. Duplicating many elements of the 1843-1845 Courthouse, the winning design called for the removal of the Courthouse's portico, construction of the present Main Street facade, and the addition of a copper cresting throughout. At present the expansion of 1898-1899 remains in original condition. A major addition built in 1954 across the rear of the Courthouse gave it ample frontage on Harvard Street. Architects for this were Stuart W. Briggs and Cornelius W. Buckley.

Worcester Memorial Auditorium
Lincoln Square

Lucius Briggs, Frederic C. Hirons (New York)

The Worcester War Memorial Auditorium, built in Lincoln Square in 1931-1932, is one of Worcester's latest and most imposing Classical Revival buildings. Set on a base of "Deer Island granite," the upper portion of the structure is faced with dressed, Indiana limestone, decorated with a variety of classical ornament much of which is stylized, bas-relief, in the manner of the Art Deco style. The facade of the building is set above three flights of stairs and consists of a base with five entries, surmounted by a monumental Doric portico. The interior of the building contains both a large auditorium and the "Little Theatre" which share a stage capable of being opened to join the rooms together. Murals in the entry hall were painted by Leon Kroll and consist of a large panel (57' x 30') depicting "people of all classes and races gathered in peace and harmony under the American flag" as well as two smaller panels (25½' x 16') depicting defense on "land, air and sea." Built to serve as a memorial to the 9,000 Worcester citizens who served in World War I, the War Memorial Auditorium is in original condition and serves as a major local landmark.

Worcester Memorial Auditorium
102-W

Worcester War Memorial
Lincoln Square

Lucius Briggs & Frederic C. Hirons, architects
C. Paul Jennewein, sculptor

Worcester War Memorial
102-W

The Worcester War Memorial, built in 1935, is located in front of the Boys Club just off-center in Lincoln Square. The Worcester War Memorial consists of a circular stone platform with a flagpole at its center. The eastern half of the platform contains a semi-circular granite bench and wall which bear bas-reliefs and inscriptions which include the names of the major battles of World War I. This Memorial was dedicated in November of 1935. It was designed and built under the supervision of the Worcester War Memorial Commission.

Worcester Boys Club
Lincoln Square

Frost, Chamberlain & Edwards

Worcester Boys Club
102-W

A three storey brick structure of Georgian Revival design, the Worcester Boys Club was built in 1928-1930. The facade is concavely curved corresponding to the street in front of it. It is divided by Ionic pilasters into six bays of equal width arranged symmetrically about a slightly wider, center modillioned cornice and balustrade at the roof. The main entry of the building is framed by an elaborate limestone surround with consoles supporting a broken, segmental pediment. Side elevations resemble the facade in their finish and details. The clubhouse was the second built for the Boys Club which had a membership of 5,300 in 1928. The building occupies part of the original site of the Salisbury mansion.

Central Church
102-W

Central Church
Salisbury Street and Institute Road
Stephen C. Earle

Central Church was designed by Stephen C. Earle and built between 1884-1885 on land purchased from Stephen Salisbury III. It is an exceptionally fine, unaltered example of Romanesque Revival architecture. Composition of elements which make up Central is close to that used in earlier Earle churches, but the details have changed from English Gothic to Romanesque. Constructed of Longmeadow sandstone, the church has a high gable and rose window facing Salisbury Street, a stone and timber-work entry porch, a square-plan tower rising to an open belfry and high hip roof, a two storey tower with conical turret, and numerous other fine details including carved stonework and stained glass. According to contemporary accounts, much of the building's interior decoration and stained glass was designed by Sarah Lyman Whitman (a student of William Morris Hunt) after the studios of John Lafarge proved too busy to carry out the commission. The ceiling consists of two intersecting sheathed barrel vaults—a considerable development which permits an unusually large opening up of ceiling with the barrel vault of the nave resting on a ceiling that slopes gradually down to a wall. The chief effect of this change is to make the spaces of the nave and the transepts flow into each other and become part of one space.

Central Church is descended from the Central Congregational Society, the city's fourth religious society, formed in 1820 as the Calvinist Church. The congregation's first church stood on Main Street, near George Street, from 1825 until 1885, when the society moved to its present location. The present church was dedicated on October 11, 1885. Additions were constructed in 1928 and 1958. Central consolidated with the Chestnut Street Congregational Church in 1982.

Worcester Historical Society
39 Salisbury Street
Barker & Nourse

The Worcester Historical Society was built in 1890-1891. The structure of Romanesque Revival style design with an asymmetrical plan dominated by a square-plan, four storey tower, the base of which is opened by granite arches and serves as the major entry. Decorative trim consists of terra cotta tiles, stained glass, and original iron railings. Organized in 1875 as the Worcester Society of Antiquity, the Worcester Historical Society was formed to encourage local antiquarian research and to preserve historical materials. The Society met in members' homes and, later, in rented space until completion of the present structure on land donated to the Society in 1890 by Stephen Salisbury III. Since 1891, the Society has used 39 Salisbury Street as its headquarters. A small addition was constructed in 1964. The Society officially changed its name in 1979 to the Worcester Historical Museum.

Worcester Historical Society
102-W

Worcester Woman's Club
102-W

Worcester Woman's Club
Salisbury and Tuckerman Streets
Josephine Wright Chapman

Designed by one of this country's earliest women architects, Josephine Wright Chapman, the Worcester Woman's Club at 10 Tuckerman Street (corner of Salisbury) was built in 1902. Her other designs include Craigie House (Harvard University), the New England Building at the Pan American Exposition, and the Woman's Club of Lynn, Mass. The Woman's Club is a four storey brick building with neo-classical decorative trim. Large circular bays at the corners flank entries on both Salisbury and Tuckerman Streets. Much of the trim is limestone including a Tuscan entry porch and balustrade, water table, moulded courses, and Ionic capitals. There is a copper cornice, plus pressed metal panels with decorative wreaths, and splayed window lintels. Except for the removal of a roofline balustrade, this handsome building is in original condition. The Worcester Woman's Club was formed in 1880. The work of the organization (membership was once limited to 750) "was divided among committees on literature, history, art, science, work and education, and social entertainment. . . ," promotion of industrial training in public schools and public kindergartens. The lot on which the building stands was donated by Stephen Salisbury II.

Worcester Boys Trade School
2 Grove Street
Frost, Briggs & Chamberlain

Worcester Boys Trade School
102-W

Built in two stages from a plan prepared in 1909, the Worcester Boys Trade School is a three storey brick building with a symmetrical facade facing Grove Street. The facade is dominated by a central pavilion of five bays with a center entry set in a limestone surround. Flanking the center section are wings (three bays wide) of slightly lower height. The facade is banded by limestone courses and mouldings, and is decorated with stucco and brick panels. Most decorative trim is simple and derived from Beaux Arts designs. The basic structure of the school is unaltered, although all sash and doors were replaced in the mid-twentieth century.

Founded by the city in 1908, this school was Worcester's first trade school. Efforts to found such a school were led by Milton P. Higgins, Sr., a teacher and industrialist, who came to Worcester in the 1860s to establish the Washburn Shops at Worcester Polytechnic Institute. Higgins, who was a founder of the Norton Company and other important local industries, travelled extensively in the early twentieth century to promote the founding of trade schools. In February 1910, the first section of the school was opened. Immediately successful, the school was doubled in size by the 1916-1917 addition which was built by the school's students with $25,000 of the construction costs donated by the estate of Milton Higgins. More recent additions to the school stand as nearly separate structures south of the original school building.

Worcester National Guard Armory
102-W

Worcester National Guard Armory
44 Salisbury Street
Fuller & Delano

  The Worcester National Guard Armory was built in 1889-1890 with a major addition to the rear erected in 1907. Fuller & Delano were the architects for both. The Armory is a four storey brick structure of symmetrical plan, consisting of a head house facing Wheaton Square (formerly Armory Square), a drill hall and three storey rear wing. Containing major Romanesque Revival style elements, the head house rises from a base course of rock-faced granite ashlar to a corbelled cornice and solid parapet. At each end of the facade is a semi-octagonal corner bay, while at the facade's center is a complex, five storey pavilion containing a broad entry arch (first storey), semi-circular bays (fourth and fifth storeys) and a central square tower (fifth storey). Originally this central tower rose slightly higher. Otherwise, the building is in its original condition. It was built at a cost of $131,991.39 to replace the earlier Waldo Street Armory (1870s) which had developed structural flaws by the mid-1880s. Upon completion, the new armory was occupied by Companies A, C & H of the First Field Artillery of the Massachusetts militia. With the approach of World War I, organizational changes were made in state and federal military administration which resulted in the purchase of the armory by the Commonwealth of Massachusetts from its original owner, the City of Worcester. The size, fine details and prominent location of the Worcester Armory make it an important local landmark.

North High School
46 Salisbury Street
Fuller & Delano (1889)
John T. Simpson (1916)

Built in 1889 from plans by Fuller and Delano, architects, North High is made up of two structures: the original two and one half storey brick school building of Romanesque Revival design, and the symmetrical three storey Classical Revival building added to the west in 1915-1916 (John T. Simpson, architect).

The original building is at the eastern end of the two. It is noteworthy for its four storey octagonal tower and arched entry both of which are trimmed with elaborately carved sandstone. Considered one of the finest public buildings of its period, this Romanesque Revival structure was designed as a grammar school and served as such until 1911 when it was converted to a high school.

Although more space was needed almost from the time of the school's founding, it was not until 1915 that North High was enlarged. The three storey western section was finished in 1916. Its major features include triple entries surmounted by consoles, balconies and balustrades, plus decorative panels, tripartite windows, and limestone trim. Developers turned both buildings into condominiums for downtown living in 1982-1983.

North High School
102-W

Worcester Art Museum
102-W

Worcester Art Museum
55 Salisbury Street

Stephen Earle (1897)
William Aldrich (1933)
Architects Collaborative (1970)
Irwin Regent (1983)

The Worcester Art Museum is a complex structure built in various stages of which the 1897 building (now largely obscured by additions) and the 1933 facade are the most significant in respect to the Lincoln and Wheaton Squares District. The present facade is of classical design faced in dressed limestone. Arranged symmetrically, the facade has a first storey (treated as a basement) with three entries at its center and end pavilions; the upper floors are framed by two storey composite pilasters which support an entablature and cornice. Set behind the 1933 wing, the high hip roof, cornice with roundels and the upper walls of the original museum building are visible.

The Worcester Art Museum was founded in 1896 by Stephen Salisbury III, who made an original founding gift of one acre of land on Salisbury Street (present site) and a fund of $100,000, half of which was to pay for the building and the other half to establish an endowment. Later, in 1897, Salisbury gave additional land. A private subscription raised an additional $50,000 for the museum. The cornerstone of the original building was laid on June 24, 1897 and formally opened on May 10, 1898. In 1898, the Museum founded a school of painting and drawing which existed in various locations (including Salisbury's former house) until the construction of the museum's 1970 wing.

The last major addition on the Tuckerman Street side (The Frances Hiatt Wing) was completed in 1983 with Irwin Regent as architect.

CHAPTER V
INSTITUTIONAL BUILDINGS PRIVATE

INSTITUTIONAL BUILDINGS—PRIVATE

As with so many prosperous industrial cities, Worcester developed a large number of charitable societies, social clubs, schools, intellectual societies, and other organizations during the mid and late nineteenth century. In many cases, land and the money for building costs were provided by one or more wealthy citizens, resulting in the construction of many substantial institutional buildings, often designed by local architects.

1887	North Worcester Aid Society	1840-95	College of the Holy Cross
1890	Odd Fellows' Home	1868-90	Worcester Polytechnic Institute
1900	Greendale Improvement Society	1887-1910	Clark University
1906	I.O.O.F.	1889-1906	Worcester Academy
1914	Masonic Temple		
1930	John Woodman Higgins Armory		

photo on page 83
John Woodman Higgins Armory

Greendale Improvement Society
480 West Boylston Street

Greendale Improvement Society
33-B

Erected in 1900, the Greendale Improvement Society Building is a two storey structure of wood frame construction. A five bay facade is dominated by a projecting pedimented central bay. The pediment of the bay is formed by a gabled roof dormer containing double windows topped by a wooden fanlight decoration reminiscent of the projecting bays found in Georgian style houses. A large classical portico extends across the first floor of the bay composed of a latticework base, six square-based classical columns and a flat, slightly overhanging roof. The right bay is formed by a square, three storey tower with triple round-arched windows in its third floor. The main roof is hipped and covered with asphalt shingles. Modillions articulate the slight overhang of the roof. Wood shingles, painted gray, cover the house and its trim is painted white.

The significance of the Greendale Improvement Society Building stems from the important role played by its members in the social and humanitarian programs in Worcester. It is a classic example of a simple building housing a 19th century organization genuinely concerned with the general welfare of its citizens: planting trees, collecting rubbish, plowing snow, and providing fire protection.

The history of the Society began on January 17, 1895 when a meeting was held to consider the formation of an organization interested in the general welfare of Greendale residents. Culmination came with the acquisition of property on which the building now stands given by the Kendrick family, a charter applied for in the name of the Greendale Village Improvement Society and approved by the Massachusetts State Legislature on April 10, 1897.

Members of the Society set out to raise funds by all means available—from bean suppers to direct solicitation. Success accompanied ground breaking on April 19, 1900. Dedication of the completed building followed in October of that year.

North Worcester Aid Society
42-C

North Worcester Aid Society
58 Holden Street

Organized in the home of Mrs. Alfred Atherton in 1874, the North Worcester Aid Society originated as a group of women who gathered during the time of the Civil War to sew clothes for war orphans. Of the original fifty-five members all were women, although men eventually became involved in the organization. Formed for "educational, charitable, benevolent, social and religious purposes," the Society met in a school building on Holden Street until 1887 when the present building was constructed on land donated by Eben Jewett. The organization worked for a time under the guidance of "City Missionaries." It operated a non-sectarian Sunday School, and provided assistance to needy residents of the area.

A simple example of Victorian architecture, the building is a one and one half storey frame structure set on a brick foundation. Decoration is extremely simple, consisting of brackets and decorative aprons in the gables. The building is presently in excellent condition, altered only by the minor addition of an entry porch. The Society still operates in the same building.

Odd Fellows' Home
40 Randolph Road
Barker & Nourse (1892, 1902)

Odd Fellows' Home
44-A

Surrounded by fields, the Odd Fellows' Home is one of several charitable homes for the aged and hospitals which were built in out-lying sections of Worcester during the nineteenth century. The building's three and one half storey central section with a five storey clock tower was begun in 1890 and opened in 1892. Although the grouped windows, rock-faced granite trim and other tower details are reminiscent of Romanesque Revival design, the largest portion of the building is undecorated except for projecting brick piers and a slight corbelling at the cornice. The structure is enclosed by a slate-covered hip roof with dormers. Located on the east wall of the original building is a two and one half storey addition built in 1902 to increase the Home's capacity of 110 residents. Bearing elements of Classical Revival architecture, this addition has a symmetrical facade, trimmed with limestone quoins, an entablature and modillioned cornice. The entrance is set behind an open Tuscan porch, above which is a stone parapet.

Land for the Home was donated by Thomas Dodge, a prominent Worcester inventor and patent lawyer, who gave eleven acres to the Odd Fellows around 1890. Shortly thereafter, Dodge donated a neighboring parcel of thirteen acres to the city to ensure "ample light and air" for the Home.

The John Woodman Higgins Armory
100 Barber Avenue
Joseph Leland (Boston)

The John Woodman Higgins Armory
44-B

The Higgins Armory is a four storey, L-shaped building built in 1930 for the Worcester Pressed Steel Company whose president was John Woodman Higgins, son of Milton Prince Higgins, Sr. Of steel frame construction, the Higgins Armory is believed to have been the first building in the United States to have an exterior formed entirely of steel and glass. The building was opened on January 12, 1931, at which time the offices of the Worcester Pressed Steel Company occupied the lower two floors while the Armory occupied the two top floors.

In 1902 John Higgins and his father bought the Worcester Ferrule and Manufacturing Company which became the Worcester Pressed Steel Company. In 1905 the company moved from Main Street to Barber Avenue where John Higgins developed a variety of stamping processes to replace earlier methods of casting steel. Varying its production from time to time, the company remained in existence until the 1970s.

While Mr. Higgins was developing his interest in modern manufacture of steel parts, he became increasingly fascinated by medieval metal working exemplified by suits of armor. He purchased eight suits of armor from the George Jay Gould collection which formed the core of the Higgins Collection. In 1927, Mr. Higgins made a trip to Europe to visit armor collections and to buy items for his own. By 1928 his collection had outgrown the space available in his house at 80 William Street, and a plan was formed to open a public museum.

In 1929-1930, Joseph Leland, a Boston architect, was asked to design a combined office-museum building in which both the collection of armor and modern manufactured products could be displayed. Mr. Higgins intended the museum "to comprise an historical library and a collection of objects illustrating the progress of the art of metal working from its earliest beginnings to the present time."

Somewhat in contrast to the modernity of his ideas about industrial design, the museum's interior is built of stone and plaster forming high, vaulted Gothic baronial halls and galleries based on Prince Eugen's Castle in Hohenwerfen, Austria from which part of the collection had come. Continued acquisition has made the Higgins Armory collection one of the largest and finest in the world.

I.O.O.F. Building
674 Main Street
Clellan W. Fisher

Designed by Clellan W. Fisher of Worcester, a former partner of Stephen Earle, the I.O.O.F. Building is an opulent example of Beaux Arts Classicism, a popular style of the early twentieth century. The facade is faced with brick laid up in a Flemish bond and trimmed with dressed limestone. Three bays wide, the facade is symmetrical, rising from a low basement to a rusticated first storey. Centered on the first storey is an elaborate limestone entry with a pediment (decorated by a shield) set on consoles with garlands. On either side of the entry at the second storey are stone balconies with original iron railings. The facade's second and third storeys are framed by three arches, above which the fourth storey contains three tripartite windows, each with a stone balcony and iron railing. At the roof is a pressed metal cornice from which modillions and cresting of acroteria have been removed. The building was constructed in 1906 by a local builder, E. J. Cross, at a cost of $110,000. Although used for storage, the I.O.O.F. Building retains nearly all of its original features.

First organized in Worcester in 1844 as the Quinsigamond Lodge No. 43, the International Order of Odd Fellows was one of several fraternal organizations in Worcester which grew to have enormous memberships in the late nineteenth and

I.O.O.F. Building
142-D

early twentieth centuries. The founders of the Quinsigamond Lodge were Joseph Coburn of Boston (a mason who was then temporarily living in Worcester while building the 1844 section of the Worcester County Courthouse) and four of Coburn's employees, also temporary residents of the city. A charter was granted to the Quinsigamond Lodge on May 1, 1844; it then met at the Masonic Hall. By 1917 the membership had risen to 3,015, broken up into six lodges, most of which met at the Main Street building. In addition the organization sponsored the formation of four Rebekah Lodges (for women) and "two encampments" with a membership of approximately 1,900 in 1918.

Masonic Temple
Ionic Avenue
George C. Halcott

Masonic Temple
142-G

 The Masonic Temple is a monumental brick building approximately four and one half storeys high with a rectangular floor plan. The structure's facade sits on a high basement and is framed by wide piers of brick laid up to give the appearance of rustication. Set between the piers are eight Ionic columns between which are windows set in blind-arch frames (first storey) and decorative brick panels (second storey). At the center is an elaborately decorated entry set in an earred architrave and surmounted by a pediment on consoles. Above the facade's columns are an entablature and cornice above which is a series of square lights, surmounted by a brick parapet. Side elevations of the building repeat much of the brickwork, cornice and moulded trim of the facade, but lack columns and decorated window surrounds. At present the Masonic Temple is in original condition.

 Freemasonry got its first foothold in Worcester in 1793 when Isaiah Thomas founded the Morning Star Lodge. As with so many other social and fraternal organizations, the Masons grew rapidly in numbers during the nineteenth century, particularly toward the turn of the century. By 1910 a committee was established to look into building new headquarters, as the Masons' temple of nearly fifty years on Pearl Street had been outgrown. Land was purchased on Mower's Avenue, now Ionic Avenue (the street name was reportedly changed due to the imposing quality of the Masonic Temple's Ionic colonnade). Construction was carried out in 1911, from plans drawn by George Halcott, the superintendent of public buildings of the City of Worcester. At the time of its completion the building contained a drill hall and banquet hall on the first floor, a "Grecian Chamber" on the second floor, an "Egyptian Chamber" on the third, and a Gothic Chapel. The heaviness of the building's details and its scale make it one of the finer examples of Classical Revival architecture in Worcester.

Worcester Polytechnic Institute
Institute Road

Established in 1865 during a boom in Worcester's economy which saw many new industries created by local inventors and which resulted in a tripling of population between 1845 and 1865, Worcester Polytechnic Institute was founded by several of the city's most prominent citizens. From 1865 until 1886, the school was named the Worcester County Free Institute of Industrial Science and offered three year courses of instruction in general science, mechanical, electrical and civil engineering.

The impetus for the school's founding came from a gift of $100,000 made by John Boynton, a tinware manufacturer. To provide a campus for the proposed school, Stephen Salisbury, II, donated a piece of land bounded by Institute, West and Boynton Streets. While Boynton Hall was being constructed, a third founding donation was made by Ichabod Washburn for the construction of the Washburn Machine Shops, the first mechanical shop to be built for a technical school in the country.

By 1900 much of the original campus was built. Since that time the school has expanded by purchase of land at the corner of Salisbury and Boynton Streets, and by the purchase of large pieces of land west of West Street. While the new parts of the campus contain many fine examples of late Gothic Revival architecture, the part of the campus of greatest architectural and historical significance is that which contains the school's pre-1900 buildings. This area's long standing importance to the founding of many local industries and to the city's development, as well as the preservation of its extremely fine Victorian buildings, make it a very important part of Worcester's heritage.

Boynton Hall, built in 1868, addition 1889, Stephen Earle, architect (1868), Earle & Fisher, architects (1889). Boynton Hall was the first building constructed for WPI after it was founded in 1865. It is believed to be the first collegiate Gothic building in the United States. Built of squared granite rubble, it is a three storey structure with a four storey clock tower surmounted by a high hip roof and iron cresting. The main body of the building is enclosed by a gambrel roof concealed on the facade by a continuous dormer with multiple gables and lancet windows. The

left photo on page 91
Boynton Hall, Worcester Polytechnic Institute

right photo on page 91
Clark Hall, Clark University

first storey facade is divided into equal sized bays by buttresses. At the west end is a rectangular plan wing enclosed by a high pitched roof with its gable facing south.

Washburn Machine Shops, built in 1868 (Elbridge Boyden, architect), additions 1880, 1887, (Stephen Earle, architect). The Washburn Shops building is a superb example of Second Empire architecture designed by a major Worcester architect. The original building (now the center of the present facade) was a two and one-half storey brick structure with a slate covered mansard roof. At the facade's center is a central pavilion consisting of an octagonal bay (which rises three and one-half storeys to an octagonal cupola) flanked by one bay on each side. Flanking the central pavilion on both sides are three bays and a one bay end pavilion. In 1880, two storey brick additions (each four bays wide) were added to the ends of the original facade. Built of pressed brick, these wings differ from the original structure only by having flat roofs. In 1887, a four storey brick addition was built on the building's north end. Recently restored, the Washburn Shops are unaltered from 1887.

Electric Magnetic Laboratory, built 1886-1890, Stephen Earle, architect. No mention of architectural excellence at WPI should be made without special reference to the Electrical Magnetic Laboratory. This is a one storey Romanesque Revival style building constructed of squared granite rubble faced with rock sandstone trimmings. The facade has simple arched windows and entryway as well as a conical corner tower. Donated by Stephen Salisbury III, the laboratory was especially built without iron to conduct delicate electrical experiments, and placed on its site so that the building's axis was oriented to the earth's magnetic meridian. At the turn of the century, vibration caused by the extension of the city trolley lines negated the building's original function. Just before World War II, the lab was used by Robert Hutchings Goddard (a WPI grad of 1908) for rocketry research sponsored by the Smithsonian Institution. Of its kind, this little building is unique both because of its architectural merit and its research history.

Salisbury Laboratories, built in 1888. Stephen Earle, architect. The Salisbury Laboratories Building is a four storey brick building containing elements of Romanesque Revival Architecture. The structure rises from a first storey of rock-faced granite (laid in a broken course) to a corbelled cornice and flat roof. On the facade the main entry is set in a two storey sandstone frame with an arched

Washburn Machine Shops
102-L-3

doorway. Decoration of upper floors is limited largely to sandstone bandings and arched window heads. The Salisbury Laboratories were built at a cost of $100,000 which was donated by Stephen Salisbury III, in memory of his father, Stephen Salisbury II. Built of what was considered fire proof construction in the nineteenth century, the Laboratory Building is virtually unaltered on the exterior except for several two storey additions built along the structure's north wall. These additions were added in the 1930s and 1940s and are built of materials similar to that of the original building.

Clark University
950 Main Street

The second graduate school to be founded in the United States, Clark University, was opened in 1889 and, until the establishment of Clark College in 1902, offered only graduate education. The school was founded by donations from Jonas G. Clark, one of the city's wealthiest citizens. In the early 1850s, Clark went to California where he laid the foundation of his great fortune. Upon his return to the east coast, Clark took up residence in New York City where he remained until around 1881 when he moved to Worcester and invested heavily in local real estate.

In 1887 Jonas Clark purchased eight acres of the present Main Street campus and a board of trustees was established to operate the school. Clark's initial founding gift included a $300,000 construction fund, a $100,000 library fund and a general endowment of $600,000. Clark also donated an additional $500,000 in real estate and $500,000 for the support of three or more professorships. Active in his support of the school until his death, Clark made additional large donations including $750,000 to increase the library fund and to pay for the construction of a library in 1900. After the settling of Clark's estate around 1900-1901, further donations brought his contribution to the school to over $4,000,000.

Clark Hall, built 1887 (Stephen Earle, architect). A four storey brick building of symmetrical plan with a first storey of rock-faced granite laid in a broken course. Upper storeys are largely undecorated except for granite belt courses, lintels, sills and arched window heads. Extending around the building above its cornice is an iron cresting. In 1924 the original upper part of the clock tower collapsed. The structure was rebuilt in the manner of the original, but to a slightly lower height. At the time of the rebuilding a granite arch and fanlight were removed from above the three windows at the tower's base.

Nearly astylistic and unlike other local university buildings of its period, Clark Hall was nominally designed by Stephen Earle of Worcester. However, Earle's biography and other sources claim that he merely advised Clark in the building's design and that Clark wished the building to be easily adapted to industrial uses, should the school fail. Containing 90 rooms originally, Clark Hall housed the university's main offices, library, gymnasium and classrooms until the early twentieth century, when separate, specialized buildings began to be constructed. Throughout the university's development, Clark Hall remained the center of its campus.

Laboratory Building, built 1888 (Stephen Earle, architect). A brick structure of irregular plan, two and three storeys high. Of utilitarian design, the building's trim is limited to stone window sills, and a stone belt course above the building's high basement. During the early twentieth century, the Laboratory Building was the site of research in rocketry which was carried out by Robert Hutchings Goddard. Goddard, who is regarded as the inventor of modern high altitude rockets, was a graduate student at Clark (1908-1911) and was associated with Clark as an instructor after 1914, becoming a full professor of physics in 1919. During his tenure, in 1926, Goddard successfully fired the world's first liquid fuel rocket at a site in nearby Auburn, Massachusetts.

Academic Building, (formerly the University Library) built 1901-1902 (Frost, Briggs & Chamberlain, architects; Norcross Brothers, builders). The Academic Building is a three storey brick building of Collegiate Gothic design. Trimmed with finely dressed limestone, the building's former facade (Main Street) is symmetrical with an arched limestone entry at its center. Above the entry is an ornate oriel with pointed-arch stone tracery and a crenellated parapet. Other windows are framed by limestone quoins and are divided internally by wooden stiles to give the appearance of having transoms. It was modelled after the library of Trinity College at Cambridge, England, designed by Sir Christopher Wren.

Academic Building Addition, (formerly the University Library addition) built 1910 (Frost, Briggs & Chamberlain, architects; Norcross Brothers, builders). Built in

Academic Building
152-B-1

the same "English Collegiate Gothic" style as the original library building of 1901-1903, the former library addition is a two and one half storey brick building of rectangular plan with its major entry on its south wall. The entry consists of a pointed arch (of limestone) surmounted by a cornice and crenellated parapet. The addition's Main Street facade is slightly asymmetrical, having a bay window at its south end only. Otherwise this elevation has symmetrically placed gables and tripartite windows set in limestone surrounds with transoms. Together, both sections of Academic Hall provide one of Worcester's finest and earliest examples of Collegiate Gothic architecture.

Worcester Academy
81 Providence Street

Worcester Academy started life in 1834 as the Worcester County Manual Labor High School by a group of Baptists seeking to establish "an academy that would give the poor boy an opportunity for liberal education." In that same year $5,000 was raised locally to allow the purchase of a 60-acre farm on the east side of Main Street (between modern Hammond and Lagrange Streets) where a chapel and a "Mansion House" were constructed. In later years, when a street was cut through this property, it was named Benefit because the purchase had been such a help to the school.

Plagued by financial difficulties in 1854, the Academy sold its Main Street campus to Eli Thayer and moved to the former headquarters of the American Antiquarian Society at the corner of Summer and Belmont Streets (slated to become the site of the Valhalla Bar and Restaurant in mid-20th century, now the site of the new Worcester Police Headquarters).

In 1869 Isaac Davis, the Academy's first president, bought the present Union Hill campus. At the time of purchase, it contained a large brick building which had been designed by the Worcester architectural firm of Boyden and Ball and built in 1852. After 1869 the building was renamed Davis Hall and became classroom and dormitory space for the school. In the mid-20th century Davis Hall was demolished and replaced by modern buildings.

The first substantial building on the Union Hill campus to be designed

left photo on page 97
Walker Hall, Worcester Academy

right photo on page 97
Fenwick Hall, College of the Holy Cross

The Megaron
155-I-1

specifically for Worcester Academy was Walker Hall (1889). It was followed by Adams Hall (1892) and Dexter Hall (1892) on the north side of the campus. With the completion of 81 Providence Street (1886-1896), Kingsley Laboratories (1897) and the Megaron (1906), the school's major building period came to an end and the campus assumed much of its present appearance. These Worcester Academy buildings preserve good examples of late Victorian institutional architecture and have continuous associations with one of the city's oldest schools.

Walker Hall, built 1889 (Fuller & Delano, architects). A two and one half storey classroom building of Romanesque Revival design, this building is of brick construction with rock-faced sandstone trim. Major features include a wide sandstone entry area, arched windows (first storey), arched windows with transoms (second storey), gabled dormers and a slate-covered hip roof.

Adams Hall, built 1892 (architect unknown). Adams Hall is a one and one half storey brick structure of rectangular plan with a high hip roof. Of late Gothic Revival design, the building's major features include a buttressed entry porch with pointed-arch entry and elaborate tracery in the entry transom, sandstone trim, window labels, and a central dormer with name plaque and carved stone finial. The building's interior contains a dining hall. Adams Hall is in unaltered condition.

Dexter Hall, built 1892 (Fuller & Delano, architects). A three and one half storey brick dormitory with a symmetrical facade (west) containing central and end pavilions. The main entry is framed by a sandstone surround of engaged Ionic columns supporting a broken pediment, behind which is a sandstone and iron railing. Other decorative trim consists of sandstone mouldings, stone panels, a wooden cornice with modillions and fanlights in gables.

81 Providence Street, built 1886-1892 (architect unknown). 81 Providence Street is a two and one half storey frame house of simple Queen Anne style design. Among the building's features are some decorative shingling, eyebrow dormers and a Tuscan entry porch with a low pediment over the entry. Built for Worcester Academy, this building's original use is unclear.

Kingsley Laboratories, built 1897 (Barker & Nourse, architects). A three storey brick building with a hip roof and central, octagonal cupola, the Kingsley Laboratory Building has a symmetrical facade, arranged about a three and one half storey pavilion. Elements of the building's design are derived from Romanesque

Revival architecture, such as its rock-faced sandstone trim, sandstone entry arch with foliate carving and arched third storey windows. The building remains in largely original condition.

The Megaron, built 1906 (architect unknown). A one storey brick structure of Romanesque Revival design, the Megaron has a symmetrical facade with evenly spaced arched windows and a gabled entry porch which bears a name plaque. The Megaron was planned as a single large room to provide a social center for the campus. Both the building's name and its intended function consciously imitated the megaron as it existed in classical antiquity.

College of the Holy Cross
Mount St. James

One of Worcester's oldest schools, Holy Cross has occupied its present campus since 1836 when Reverend James Fitton bought the 60-acre farm of "Henry Patch, deceased" on Pakachoag Hill. Soon after the purchase Fitton, who had organized Worcester's first Roman Catholic Church, hired Tobias Boland, a local builder, to construct a wooden building on the property which then became the Seminary of Mount Saint James. In 1842 Fitton transferred title to Bishop Benedict Fenwick, Boston's second Roman Catholic bishop, who sought the aid of Jesuit priests from Georgetown College in Washington, D.C. to help establish a curriculum. In 1843 a brick and granite academy building was begun on the site of Fenwick Hall, and a seven year course of study was instituted. Entering students ranged in age from eight to fourteen years. Upon its completion in 1844, the original brick building contained all of the school's offices, classrooms and dormitory rooms. After the building was largely destroyed in 1852, it appeared that the school might close. Soon thereafter, the burnt building was refinanced and reconstructed.

From 1849 until 1865, Holy Cross was unchartered by the Commonwealth of Massachusetts to grant academic degrees. During this period degrees were granted through Georgetown College. In 1865 Holy Cross was chartered, apparently due to an easing of anti-Catholic sentiments which followed the Civil War. From the school's founding until the addition of O'Kane Hall in 1895, Fenwick Hall housed nearly all of the college's activities. After 1904, when other buildings began to be added to the campus, Fenwick and O'Kane lost some of their earlier functions, but remained the school's major buildings.

Fenwick Hall, portions of east wing built 1840s; portions built 1852-1853 (Capt. Edward Lamb, architect); enlargement and extensive rebuilding 1867 (Elbridge Boyden, architect); enlargement 1875 (P. W. Ford, architect); "Commencement Porch" added 1907.

Fenwick Hall is a three and one half storey brick structure (approximately 310' x 50') bearing elements of Victorian Gothic, Second Empire and Classical Revival styles due to the building's many additions and re-designings carried out in the nineteenth and very early twentieth centuries. The building is symmetrical in plan with a central pavilion from which rise two towers, and end pavilions with two storey high hip roofs. Fenestration of the facade is asymmetrical consisting mostly of evenly spaced windows at each storey except at the second and third storeys of the structure's east end, where there are two storey lancet windows. Except for the towers, the building is enclosed by a mansard roof with evenly spaced, arched dormers. At the center of the facade is a two storey Corinthian portico added in 1907. Additions so changed the original Fenwick Hall that in 1893 the *Worcester Commercial Magazine* commented: "Few traces of the original building remain; the transformation has been so perfect that but a small part of the first foundations have been left undisturbed."

O'Kane Hall, built 1895 (Fuller & Delano, architects). Attached to the west-end wall of Fenwick Hall, O'Kane Hall is a five storey brick structure of symmetrical plan, arranged about a central tower and end pavilions. Containing elements of Romanesque Revival and Renaissance Revival styles, the building's facade is dominated by a square-plan tower which rises in stages to a high pyramidal roof and pinnacles. The facade's fenestration consists mainly of regularly spaced windows except for the southern end of the third and fourth storeys where two storey arched windows provide light to an auditorium. At the building's north end is a six storey, flat-top tower which was designed (as was the central facade tower) to harmonize with the towers of Fenwick Hall. At the rear of O'Kane is a circular-plan tower, five storeys high with a conical roof. In addition to its auditorium, O'Kane Hall was designed to contain a gymnasium, assembly halls and classrooms.

O'Kane Hall
178-A-1

CHAPTER VI
INDUSTRIAL
BUILDINGS
& DISTRICTS

INDUSTRIAL BUILDINGS

Although Worcester's present industrial districts appear in scattered locations, much of the apparent discontinuity results from recent demolitions rather than from erratic original siting. Prior to the mid-twentieth century, the largest number of the city's factories existed slightly east of the commercial district in an arc which roughly followed the course of the former Mill Brook and Blackstone Canal. Beginning at its north end with the Washburn and Moen North Works on Grove Street, this arc extended southward along Union and Summer Streets to Washington Square from which it extends southward to Harding, Winter and Green Streets before terminating north of Kelley Square. Containing some of the city's earliest and most important factories, this area (having been the location of urban renewal efforts and highway construction) now contains only fragmented remains. A second industrial district exists south of Madison Street along the tracks of the Norwich, Worcester, and New York Central Railroad beds. This district extends southward along Beacon and Tainter Streets to Grand Street, and along Southbridge Street to Armory Street. A secondary branch of this district extends southward on Quinsigamond Avenue to Cambridge Street. Additional industrial districts exist southeast of Webster Square (on Cambridge and Webster Streets), on Park Avenue south of Pleasant Street, and south of Shrewsbury Street near the New York Central Railroad bed.

At present no reliable estimates are available for the number of factory buildings which remain; however, production statistics for 1913 note the presence of 448 separate manufacturing establishments, while later statistics for 1917, a boom year, note that more than 500 factories in Worcester produced $100,000,000 worth of goods. Despite widespread demolitions, many factories built between 1890 and 1930 remain. Of the total number of factories remaining, an extremely small number (less than fifty structures) pre-date 1890, many having been demolished in the early

photo on page 101
Employees of the Washburn and Moen North
  Works (1874)
courtesy of Harvard Business School

twentieth century to be replaced by larger buildings. Because of the limited number of these earlier factories, their architectural individuality, and the associations to the formation of local industry, they form the bulk of industrial buildings included in this book. Factories built between 1890 and 1930 are included here when they form part of a cohesive industrial district; however, the large number that remain, their architectural uniformity and associations with the corporate state of local industry make their historical significance less clear-cut at present than that of the earlier factories.

North Works (1863–1916)
Washburn and Moen Manufacturing Company
Grove Street

Headquarters for the Washburn and Moen Manufacturing Co. during the 19th century, the North Works along Grove Street developed into one of Worcester's largest industrial complexes. Major growth took place between 1863 and 1870. Although some of the Second Empire style decorative detailing has been removed, the majestic Grove Street facade with its central tower and extreme length (over 500 feet) still dominates the area as an imposing corporate symbol. The Prescott Street buildings of more utilitarian design form a continuous band of brick factories.

The Main Building near the center of the Grove Street complex was built in 1870. The brick frontage is of symmetrical plan with a concave facade dominated at its center by a pavilion which rises above the cornice. Flanking the pavilion on each side are five bays of equal width and a narrow, slightly projecting pavilion at each end of the facade. The center pavilion contains a major entrance at its center enlarged in the 20th century. Fenestration of the main body consists of evenly spaced windows with ornamented caps (1st and 2nd storeys) and brick heads (3rd and 4th storeys). Above the fourth floor is a corbelled brick cornice.

In all, the North Works includes three groups of buildings and one small detached building built between 1863 and the early 1930s. The area occupies a trapezoidal shaped lot bounded on the west by Grove Street, on the east by

North Works
Washburn and Moen Manufacturing Company
89-U

Prescott Street, on the north by modern warehouses (occupying the site of a Washburn and Moen barbed wire factory), and on the south by parking lots where once stood the company's annealing house.

The origins of Washburn and Moen date back to 1831 when Ichabod Washburn and Benjamin Goddard, lead pipe and machinery manufacturers, developed a wire-drawing process which could draw an iron rod 15 feet through a die in one step, drastically reducing the time then needed to make wire. By 1833 the business had outgrown their mill at Northville (Millbrook Street area, Worcester). They leased land and water rights at "The Grove" (now Grove Street) from Stephen Salisbury II, who provided materials and paid for labor to build Washburn and Goddard's first mill in 1834 on the site of the North Works. A year later Washburn bought out Goddard's interest. In 1850 Ichabod formed the I. Washburn and Moen Wire Works with his son-in-law, Philip Moen.

"Firsts" became run-of-the-mill for the new company which was the first American manufacturer of telegraph wire (1847), first successful developer of a gauge to measure wire size (1849), first to patent a continuous wire tempering process (1850), first to make piano wire (1851). In 1857 Washburn invented a new process for hardening and tempering wire continuously. During the 1860s the company became a major producer of crinoline wire for hoop skirts.

In 1868 Washburn suffered a stroke forcing merger of his two companies (I. Washburn and Moen Wire Works and the Quinsigamond Wire Works) into Washburn and Moen Manufacturing Co. 1869 saw the Worcester installation of the nation's first continuous wire-rod rolling mill. Automatic machinery for making barbed wire came in 1876 and played an important part in the settling of the West. In 1879 the company began producing wire nails. With the increasing importance of electricity, Washburn and Moen became a major producer of electrical wire and cable, copper wire for telephones (1884), and insulated wire (1890).

Washburn and Moen was absorbed by American Steel & Wire in 1899 which in turn became a part of U.S. Steel in 1901. From that time on Worcester plants became specialty producing units. In 1943, the North Works was abandoned in favor of newer facilities at the South Worcester Quinsigamond factories. Today, the buildings of the old North Works on Grove Street serve a diverse group of commercial and small manufacturing interests. Several are still turning out wire products.

A listing of the structures contained in this District appears on page 116.

Salisbury Factory Buildings (1879, 1882)
25 and 49-51 Union Street
Elbridge Boyden (25 Union Street)
Stephen Earle (49-51 Union Street)

Extending along the east side of Union Street, south from Lincoln Square, is an area once known as the Union Street Manufacturing District. It consisted of a cluster of factories built for investment by the Salisbury family and leased to various businesses. Prior to 1960, this area was part of a continuous factory complex, the city's oldest, located slightly east of Main Street and the central business district. Of this once extensive factory grouping, only pockets remain.

During the 18th century, the land in this area was part of a farm owned by Stephen Salisbury I. About 1829 his son, Stephen II, began the district's major period of industrial development with the construction of the Court Mills (now demolished) near the site of the present Police Station. Planned as rental properties, these mills were the first in Worcester to provide rental space and power for small manufacturers. The success of this system of ownership, which freed small companies from the expense of owning property, set the pattern for Worcester's industrial development. This development was dominated by small firms based on their founder's inventions, rather than by several large concerns as was the case in Lowell and Lawrence. Throughout the 19th century, the Salisburys played a major role in Worcester's industrial expansion by building factories to accommodate the city's growing industry.

As business grew in these rented quarters, some firms went on to build their own factories, while others moved into larger quarters built to order by the Salisburys. 25 and 49-51 Union Street were among these.

25 Union Street is a five storey brick building adjacent to the Police Station in Lincoln Square. Designed by Elbridge Boyden and constructed by H. W. Eddy, it was one of two identical factories (the second was torn down) built next to each other for Stephen Salisbury III, between 1896 and 1899 on the site of the old Court Mills. Bearing simple trim, the facade displays Victorian Gothic elements in its buff sandstone string courses, corbelling, parapet and bracketed entry hood. Side walls are unornamented and have evenly spaced windows of 9/9 sash set in brick

surrounds with arched heads. Alterations in 1978-1979 consist of a brick elevator shaft (north wall), modern single pane sash (fourth storey), and a minor five storey addition (southeast corner).

25 Union Street was built for the use of the Munroe Organ Reed Company which occupied the building until 1889 when it was taken over by Porter & Gardner who were manufacturers of lasts. In 1903, the factory was sold by Mr. Salisbury and has since been occupied by a succession of small firms. Today it houses a restaurant and club, plus two small businesses.

49-51 Union Street at the northeast corner of Union and Market Streets was designed by Stephen Earle and built in 1882 for Stephen Salisbury III. Originally trapezoidal in plan, it had an ell at its northeast corner. The original portion is three storeys high with a flat roof, corbelled cornice, parapet (west facade) and undecorated granite trim. Between 1886 and 1896, a two storey brick addition was made to the building's Union Street side. Also designed by Earle, this addition included the structure's present double entry which is capped by a heavy granite hood set on granite consoles.

Built for the Worcester Barbed Wire Fence Company, founded in 1881 by Thomas H. Dodge (a local patent lawyer and inventor who held patents on textile, paper-making and agricultural machinery) and by Charles Washburn, the company was loosely connected with the Washburn & Moen Manufacturing Company of which Charles' uncle, Ichabod, had been a founder. In 1883, Mr. Dodge was forced by ill health to retire from business, resulting in the purchase of the Worcester Barbed Wire Company by Washburn & Moen which already held many barbed wire patents and was the largest producer of barbed wire in the U.S. Use of the factory for wire manufacture continued until 1898 after which the building was rented by George L. Brownell, an inventor and maker of twisting machinery for the manufacture of diverse materials ranging from silk thread to heavy rope. In 1909 Mr. Brownell's business expanded to occupy the entire building which he had purchased from Stephen Salisbury's estate in 1908. 49-51 is today part of Union place rented to a variety of small enterprises.

Salisbury Factory Building
25 Union Street
117-A-1

Hammond Organ Reed Factory (1870s–1880s)
9 May Street

Hammond Organ Reed Factory
141-NN

The former Hammond Organ Reed Factory is a Second Empire style brick building of two storey height with a basement and a third storey beneath its slate-covered mansard roof. The plan is irregular, reflecting the various additions made to its north and west walls during the 1870s and 1880s. The facade is on May Street and has an off-center entrance which is approached from a high granite stoop. Extending along May Street is an original cast-iron fence, set in a granite base.

One of the few remaining Second Empire style factory buildings in Worcester, the Hammond Factory was built for Andrew Hammond (1830-1906), a native of New Hampshire who worked as an "iron moulder" in Manchester and Laconia, New Hampshire before coming to Worcester in 1851. Having worked at the malleable iron works of Waite, Chadsey & Co., as well as at several local foundries, Hammond found the work "distasteful" and turned to the study of music. He traveled briefly as a music teacher in the American West before returning to Worcester and entering the organ reed firm of Edward Harrington and Augustus Rice, of which Hammond became sole owner in the 1860s. In 1868 Hammond built the easternmost portion of the May Street factory. Additions were made until it reached its present size by 1886 when more than 200 workers were employed there. Between the 1890s and World War I, the plant was believed to be the largest organ reed factory in the world. In recent years, a portion of the building has been covered with aluminum siding.

The Junction Shop
142-B

The Junction Shop Manufacturing District (1821–1925)

Just west of a major railroad junction formed by the Boston and Maine and the New York, New Haven & Hartford, the Junction Shop Manufacturing District contains one of Worcester's greatest concentrations of 19th century factory buildings, most of which remain unaltered.

The Junction Shop itself, built in 1851, is the oldest known mill building extant in Worcester. The largest of several mills constructed for Col. James Estabrook and Charles Wood in an area bounded by Jackson, Beacon and Hermon Streets, this district was known as the Junction. Concealed from street view by factories of a later period, the Junction Shop is a three storey stone structure faced with stucco 450 feet long by 50 feet wide.

It was modelled after two well-known earlier mills (now demolished) built by Stephen Salisbury II (the Court Mills) and William T. Merrifield (the Merrifield Building) to provide space for small manufacturers with steam power for manufacturing—an unusual facility for those days which saved young firms from having to make major investments in building and machinery prior to developing their businesses.

In 1879, the Knowles Loom Works began to occupy space in the Junction Shop. The firm, which manufactured looms invented by its founders, Lucius J. and Francis B. Knowles, began in Worcester in 1866. Although additions were made to the Junction Shop to accommodate the growing business, in 1890 the company was incorporated and moved to its own, larger factory on Grand Street where it became Crompton & Knowles Loom Works.

During the 1890s a major portion of the Junction Shop was occupied by the Cereal Machine Company. Founded by Henry D. Perky, a proponent of natural foods, the company remained here until 1902, when the availability of cheap water power and proximity to grain-growing areas led the company to move its plant to Niagara Falls, New York.

Although on a somewhat smaller scale, other factories in the District provided rental space for small manufacturers, corset and thread companies.

A listing of the structures contained in this District appears on page 116.

Southbridge-Sargent Manufacturing District (1866, 1892)

The Southbridge-Sargent Manufacturing District is located immediately east of the junction of the Boston and Albany, the Norwich and Worcester, and the New York, New Haven and Hartford Railroads. The construction of these railroad beds in the mid-nineteenth century led to the development of the surrounding area as one of Worcester's major manufacturing centers, known as The Junction. Having developed into a densely built industrial district by the early twentieth century, The Junction remained an active center of manufacturing until the mid-twentieth century when the decline of the city's center, and the departure of many firms, brought about the demolition of many factories which left the area with only fragmented remains of its industrial past. Containing three factories, the district has historical associations with two major local industries: the manufacture of machine cards for the textile industry and the manufacture of building materials. Particularly important is the Sargent Card-Clothing Factory (300 Southbridge Street), one of Worcester's earliest remaining factory buildings and a unique example of a once important building type. The other two factories (Rice and Griffin Manufacturing Company, 5 Sargent Street—machine cards; and Whitcomb Manufacturing Company, 125 Gold Street—building materials) are of more utilitarian design.

Built in 1866, the Sargent Card-Clothing Factory is one of the most architecturally significant factory buildings in Worcester. The structure is built of brick, two storeys high with a third storey enclosed by a mansard roof. The walls are divided by piers into even bays, each of which rises to a corbelled head and corbelled cornice. Centered in the building's west end is a square-plan tower which runs to four storeys (original hip-on-hip roof removed in the 20th century). On its west face the tower contains the building's major entry, a date plaque, and a name plaque. The tower's north, west and south elevations are framed by corner piers which support blind arches at the fourth storey. Set within each arch is a single oculus. The Sargent Factory's plan and details are characteristic of a large number of factories built in Worcester during the last half of the 19th century, including the first factories built for the use of individual firms. Subsequent demolitions of earlier factory buildings have left the Sargent Factory and the Ashworth and Jones

Southbridge-Sargent Manufacturing District
142-C

Factory as the only well-preserved examples of their type.

In 1866, Joseph B. and Edward Sargent, brothers, whose father operated a successful card-clothing factory in Leicester, formed the Sargent Card-Clothing Company and built 300 Southbridge Street. By 1881, the firm was among the largest of its type in the United States, manufacturing "Machine Cards for Cotton, Wool and Flax machinery." In 1890 the business was sold to the American Card Clothing Company, a conglomerate which purchased all but two card-clothing factories in the United States. Still in use for industrial purposes, the Sargent Factory is an important survivor of Worcester's industrial past.

Crompton Loom Works (1860)
132-142 Green Street

Crompton Loom Works
143-C

With sections dating from 1860, the former Crompton Loom Works is among the oldest factory buildings in Worcester and has important historical associations with one of Worcester's largest industries. Although the company was not founded until 1851, the invention of the first power loom capable of weaving fancy goods (upon which its initial success was based) was patented by William Crompton in 1836, the same year in which he first came to the United States. Crompton, a native of Lancashire, England, returned to England in 1837 and was successful in introducing his looms into English cotton manufacturing.

By 1840, Crompton had returned to Worcester where he manufactured looms until a fire destroyed his factory in 1845. Between 1845 and 1848, Crompton lived in Millbury, Mass. and Hartford, Conn.; by 1849 he had become "mentally incapacitated for business" and never again was active in manufacturing. His son, George, sought and was granted an extension of his father's patent rights until 1858. As a result of this extension, George Crompton formed a partnership with Merrill Furbush in 1851. Together, the two manufactured looms at the Merrifield building until it was destroyed by fire in 1854. Shortly after this fire, the firm rented space at the "Red Mills" which Crompton bought in 1860 and demolished to make way for the center section of the present structure.

In 1859, Furbush withdrew from the business which then remained under George Crompton's direction until his death in 1886. During this period the

A listing of the structures contained in this District appears on page 116.

business expanded rapidly, resulting in major additions to the Green Street factory. Among the firm's most famous inventions was a broad loom, designed by George Crompton in 1857, which quadrupled the productivity of his father's earlier power loom and which caused manufacturers to abandon narrow cassimere looms in favor of the more productive broad looms. Crompton was awarded the only medal given for textile machinery at the Paris Exposition of 1867 for this loom. In the 1870s, he obtained patents on improvements to the design of the Keighley dobby loom which he introduced into the United States. He also invented the Crompton gingham loom during this period.

By 1897, the firm had merged with its chief competitor to form the Crompton and Knowles Loom Works. In 1900, the Cromptons sold their interest in the company. After 1915, the company ceased production at the Green Street factory, although it remained a major local industry.

The Crompton Loom Works is a complex factory building, the result of many additions built by the Crompton Loom Works and by the Crompton and Knowles Loom Works. The earliest section of the building stands south of the present tower and was built in 1860. This structure was two storeys high with a deep gabled pavilion at its center and smaller, flanking end pavilions with arched gables. Between 1881 and 1886, the roof of the south end pavilion was removed while that of the north end pavilion was replaced by an extra storey and a high hip roof, creating the tower on the Green Street facade. At the same time the building was extended northward where it ended in a three storey pavilion with hip roof. Some time after 1888, a third storey was added to the entire structure, replacing the original gabled roof and bringing the building to its present appearance.

Harding and Winter Streets Manufacturing District (1870–1910)

Immediately east of the former Blackstone Canal bed (which was filled in to create Harding Street in the 1850s), the Harding and Winter Streets Manufacturing District was a major local center of boot and shoe manufacturing contained in a group of three to six storey brick factory buildings built between 1870 and 1898—all of utilitarian design. The shoe industry became the city's third largest by 1885. Of the 2650 people employed in the district that year, nearly a quarter worked in

Harding and Winter Streets Manufacturing District
143-G-1

Adriatic Mill
165-C

the Heywood and Walker factories. Even after the sale of the Walker Company, the area remained Worcester's largest shoe manufacturing center due to the continued growth of the Heywood Company. In the early 1890s, the construction of the Hill Envelope factory brought to the area one of the city's largest and oldest envelope makers. After the closing of the Walker Company, and during the 1890s, a number of small businesses located in the area providing a variety of businesses characteristic of the city's pattern of industrial development. Companies best known to this area included: J. H. & G. M. Walker Shoe, S. R. Heywood Company, Hill Envelope Company (later to become U. S. Envelope Company), Abraham Israel Factory (underwear manufacturer), and Worcester Stained Glass Works.

The construction of Interstate Route 290 in the 1970s and the decline of manufacturing in Worcester's center have left this district fragmented. Nevertheless, all of its nineteenth century factories are intact preserving the atmosphere of many of Worcester's now vanished industrial quarters.

Adriatic Mill (1854)
3-35 Armory Street

Built by Congressman Eli Thayer in 1854, the Adriatic Mill is the second oldest mill in Worcester (the Junction Shop, 1851, was the first). Located between 3 and 35 Armory Street, the mill was used as a pistol factory from 1859 to 1861, then as an army barracks until 1863 when Jordan Marsh Company of Boston established it as a woolen mill. Eventually it became the Worcester Woolen Mills which went out of business in 1928. Presently, the mill contains the original 1854 structure which is a two storey building, 400 feet long, constructed of stone chips covered with stucco. It is now owned and operated by the Standard Foundry Division of the Chromalloy Corporation.

Thayer was principal of Worcester Academy from 1847-1854. In 1849 he founded Oread Collegiate Institute in Worcester, the country's second institution of higher education for women, and was the designer of its eccentric Gothic Revival building, now demolished. He entered politics in the 1850s. In later life, he pursued development of his large real estate holdings, including the Adriatic Mill, which he is reported to have built as an investment and which he rented prior to its sale to the Joslyn Pistol Company in 1859.

A listing of the structures contained in this District appears on page 116.

Ashworth & Jones Company (1870)
1511 Main Street

Ashworth & Jones Factory
173-B

    Located on a section of Kettle Brook which had been used for textile manufacturing from the early 19th century, the Ashworth & Jones factory is among Worcester's finest examples of 19th century industrial architecture. The main section of the factory was built in 1870 and is a three storey brick structure measuring 50 feet wide by 170 feet long. Characteristic of many mills built in Worcester between 1850 and the 1880s, of which few examples remain, the Ashworth & Jones mill has an entry bell tower centered on its facade. This tower contains loading platforms and a mansard roof with dormers. Walls of the original section are divided into bays by brick piers which rise to corbelled heads and a cornice supported by paired brackets. Except for a small brick addition on the northwest side of the tower and loading bays on its west wall, this section of the mill is virtually intact. Between 1878 and 1886 one and two storey additions were built northeast of the original mill. Employing the same system of bays as the original mill, these additions may have contained company offices. Further additions between 1886 and 1896 were made again using the same brick construction as that of the original mill, although this second set of additions was only two storeys high. The factory's most recent section dates from 1900-1915. Of utilitarian brick construction, it is three storeys high.

    Thomas Ashworth immigrated to the United States in 1845, and operated one of the country's first shoddy mills in Holden by 1856. In 1861, Ashworth and Edward Jones formed a partnership and purchased a mill privilege on the Kettle Brook at Valley Falls (site of the present building). In 1870 the firm built the initial section of the present factory which was operated by Ashworth and Jones until the deaths of Ashworth (1882) and Jones (1885) after which the business was sold to E. D. Thayer. Thayer expanded the mills and manufactured woolens here until his death in 1907. In 1910 Thayer's heirs sold the business to George E. Duffy who further expanded the mill for the manufacture of "overcoatings and cloakings."

Whittall Mills
165-C

Whittall Mills (1870–1930)

Located on a former mill privilege, bounded by Crompton and Southbridge Streets, the Middle River and the N.Y., N.H., and Hartford Railroad, the Whittall Mills were built between 1870 and 1930 as the major center of Worcester's large carpet industry. Industrial use of the site dates from at least 1824 when a machine shop here was owned by White & Boyden. The district's major significance, however, post-dates 1870, the year in which the Crompton Carpet Company was formed.

Founded by George Crompton (owner of the Crompton Loom Works) and Horace Wyman, the Crompton Carpet Company was the second American firm to possess power looms for the manufacture of Brussels carpets (the first was the Bigelow Company of Clinton, Mass.). At a time when restrictive English patent laws hindered the importation of looms, Crompton and Wyman invented their own power loom. In 1870-1872 the company built the Packachoag Mill and equipped it with 16 Crompton looms which were powered by the neighboring Middle River.

In 1879 the property and its machinery (then containing 36 Crompton looms) were leased to William J. Hogg of Philadelphia. Hogg continued to rent the property until 1884, when a fire destroyed much of the Packachoag Mills. He then bought and rebuilt the factory as a yarn mill and began manufacturing carpets in partnership with his father as William James Hogg & Company, later changed to Worcester Carpet Company. In 1893 a second mill was constructed and water rights to the adjoining Stillwater Pond (now filled) were purchased from George Crompton, who had created the pond in the 1870s. The Middle River continued to be an important source of power for the Worcester Carpet Mills, even after their purchase by Matthew J. Whittall between 1901 and 1906.

The individual most responsible for the Whittall Mills development was Matthew J. Whittall, an English immigrant, who worked in the 1870s as superintendent of the Crompton Carpet Mill. In 1874 Whittall travelled to England and returned to Worcester with 8 Crossley Carpet Looms which he set up in rented loft space elsewhere in the city. The expansion of Whittall's business led to the addition of 8 more looms in 1882 and to the purchase of land facing the Packachoag Mill, on which Whittall Mill #1 was built in 1883. In 1884 Whittall expanded his original mill and rebuilt part of the Packachoag Mill as a yarn mill. Continued successes were celebrated with the erection of six new buildings between 1889 and 1910, plus major additions to five existing mills.

It is likely that a large number of these buildings and alterations were designed by Stephen Earle, who designed at least one factory here in the 1880s, and who, in the 1890s, designed Whittall's own house (nearby on Southbridge Street, now demolished) and St. Matthew's Church.

By 1906 the company's large size led to the formation of Whittall Associates of which Matthew J. Whittall was president and treasurer until his death, and Matthew P. Whittall was assistant treasurer. By World War I, the Whittall Mills contained more than 500,000 square feet of floor space, 350 looms and employed 1500 skilled laborers.

By far the largest employer in South Worcester, the Whittall Mills increased the speed of residential development in that area, particularly during the 1880s and 1890s. The Whittall Company continued to manufacture carpets here until the company was sold in 1950.

A listing of the structures contained in this District appears on page 116.

Washburn and Moen North Works
buildings include:

Cotton Mill, 1863
Long Mill, 1869
Annealing House #10, 1869
Machine Shop, 1869-70
Main Building, 1870
Gate Way, 1870
Annealing House #14, 1870
Quartermaster, ca. 1870
Machine Shop #23, 1878, 1886
Wire Mill #4, 1878, 1886
Rolling Mill #17, 1870s
Unnamed Structure, 1870s
Addition, 1916

The Junction Shop Manufacturing District
includes buildings at:

The Junction Shop, 1851
Additions to Junction Shop, 1880s and 1890s
17 Herman Street, 1865, 1870
21 Herman Street, 1890s
23-25 Herman Street, ca. 1869
33 Herman Street, 1872
35 Herman Street, 1888
47 Herman Street, 1877-1881
53 Herman Street, ca. 1879
54-56 Herman Street, 1870s
57 Herman Street, ca. 1878
29 Jackson Street, 1880s
51-53 Jackson Street, 1890s
57 Jackson Street, 1880s
59 Jackson Street, 1880s
62-64 Beacon Street (also 49-51 Herman Street), 1870s
66-68 Beacon Street, 1870s
70-74 Beacon Street, 1870s
73 Beacon Street, 1913
75 Beacon Street, 1880s
76 Beacon Street, 1890s

79 Beacon Street, 1890s
81 Beacon Street, 1911-1922
Unnamed Structure, 1880s

Southbridge-Sargent Manufacturing District
includes buildings at:

300 Southbridge Street, 1866
5 Sargent Street, ca. 1890
134 Gold Street, 1892

Harding and Winter Streets Manufacturing District includes buildings at:

63-65 Winter Street, 1895
69 Winter Street, 1870
68-80 Winter Street, 1879
73 Winter Street, 1870
82-88 Winter Street, 1879
28 Water Street, 1870
48 Water Street, 1890

Whittall Mills buildings include:

Main Offices, 1910
Power House (first), 1903
Power House (second), 1930
Whittall Mill #1, 1883
Whittall Mill #2, 1889
Whittall Mill #3, 1891-1905
Worcester Carpet Mill #1, 1870s
Worcester Carpet Mill #2, 1893-1906
Packachoag Mill, 1870-71
Edgeworth Mill, 1889
Dye House, 1904
Wool Storage, 1905
Shop, ca. 1920s
General Storehouse, 1920
Central Building, 1920s

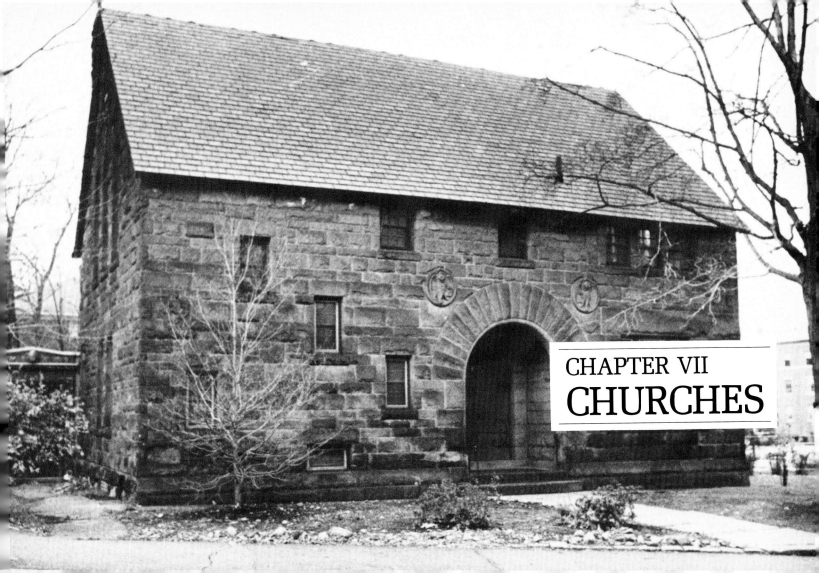

CHAPTER VII
CHURCHES

CHURCHES

Although no early meetinghouses or pre-1840 church buildings remain, Worcester contains more than 100 church buildings which pre-date World War I. Those located in outlying, suburban neighborhoods tend to be wooden construction and are owned by relatively small congregations which formed as the city grew. Toward the center of the city, particularly around Main Street between Lincoln Square and Webster Square, there exist a large number of brick and stone churches, representing various Victorian architectural styles. These are of exceptionally high architectural quality. Well-preserved examples range in style from early "Norman Romanesque" of the 1850s to Victorian Gothic of the 1860s and 1870s and Romanesque Revival of the 1880s and 1890s. A particularly large number of fine Romanesque Revival style churches remain, designed by Stephen Earle and many built by the Norcross Brothers.

St. John Catholic Church (1845) is the city's oldest church building and is associated with the establishment of Catholicism in central Massachusetts. Now covered with aluminum siding, the Holy Trinity Armenian Apostolic Church, although designed by Stephen Earle, is more important for its role as the first Armenian Church in the United States than for its architecture. Contrarily, two other buildings which are architecturally significant Worcester landmarks, the First Unitarian Church, part of the Lincoln-Wheaton Square District, and All Saints Episcopal Church, have undergone reconstruction which renders them ineligible for National Register listing.

photo on page 117
St. Mark's Episcopal Church

1845	St. John Church		1887	Pilgrim Congregational Church
1853	Main Street Baptist Church		1888	St. Mark's Episcopal Church
1854	Mission Chapel		1894	St. Matthew's Episcopal Church
1869	Cathedral of St. Paul		1894	South Unitarian Church
1884	St. Peter's Church		1895	Union Congregational Church

For information on Central Church, see Institutional District, page 76.

Union Congregational Church
5 Chestnut Street
Earle & Fisher

Designed by Stephen Earle and Clellan Fisher, and built between 1895-97, Union Congregational Church is a major local example of Gothic Revival architecture. Reminiscent on a small scale of Notre Dame de Paris, the church's major facade is flanked by two matching towers which rise to open landings formed by paired pointed arches with crenellated parapets and gargoyles above. Set between the towers an entry porch made up of three trefoil arches at the ground level, above which are a large rose window and an open arcade of trefoil arches which connects the two towers. Until 1954, an ornate copper-clad spire rose to a height of 180 ft. over the crossing of the church's nave and transept. Major structural weakness necessitated its removal. Immediately south of the church is the Moen Chapel and parish house, both original to the 1895 design. Although smaller in scale than the church, the Moen Chapel shares the same decorative elements of pointed arch windows, trefoil lights, buttresses and an entry porch formed by a trefoil arch. With the exception of the removal of its spire the church is well preserved, retaining abundant stained glass and carved stone ornament.

Formed as the Union Congregational Church in 1835 by members of the First Congregational Church of Worcester and the Second (Calvinist) Church of Worcester, a meetinghouse was built later on Front Street at the corner of Commercial. The meetinghouse was enlarged in 1845 and again in 1861 to accommodate a growing congregation. In 1894 a committee was established to consider sites for a new church. In February 1895, the site of the present building (formerly the Kinnicutt Estate) was purchased and ground broken in July 1895. While the church was under construction, the Salem Street Church merged with the Union Church.

In 1936 it became Chestnut Street Congregational Church as a result of mergers with Union, Piedmont, and Plymouth. In 1982 Chestnut and Central consolidated with Chestnut's congregation moving to the Central Church building. The Chestnut Street Church is now privately owned.

Union Congregational Church
130-C

Cathedral Church of St. Paul
38 Chatham Street
E. Boyden & Son

Cathedral Church of St. Paul
130-M

Begun in 1868 and completed (with the exception of its tower) in 1874, the Cathedral Church of St. Paul is perhaps Worcester's finest Victorian Gothic church building. The church has a traditional plan of nave and transept with covered side aisles. The building's major facade is asymmetrical with a square-plan tower, gable with pointed arch windows, and a secondary tower with stone turret. The major tower rises in stages with buttresses at its corners. Above the ridge of the nave this tower has a belfry formed by pointed arches. Also on the facade is an open porch made up of pointed arches set in polished granite columns. The side walls of the church are divided into bays of equal size each containing a pointed arch window at the ground level and a smaller one at the clerestory. St. Paul's was designed by Worcester architect, Elbridge Boyden, constructed of gray granite, and cost $200,000 to build. In 1889 the tower was completed, based on Boyden's original plans.

St. Paul's Parish was formed by Father John Power, rector of St. Anne's Parish, who purchased the site of St. Paul's Church in 1866. A building fund was established in 1867 and the basement of the present building completed in 1869. Services were held in the basement beginning July 4, 1869, until the main church hall was completed. By 1889 the congregation had grown to 3600 members. Land neighboring the church was gradually purchased. In 1906 a women's home was founded, in 1912 a parochial school was opened, and in 1914 a convent was completed. At the height of the church's activity, its property housed more than three hundred people in its homes for women, "working girls," and orphans.

In 1903 the interior of the church underwent a redecoration, thought to have cost $100,000. According to contemporary accounts, a main altar of white marble, bronze gates for the sanctuary, sculpted stations of the Cross and gold mosaic tiles in the sanctuary were all added at this time. A more recent modernization of the interior, including addition of new stained glass windows, was carried out in the late 1960s.

The Mission Chapel
205 Summer Street

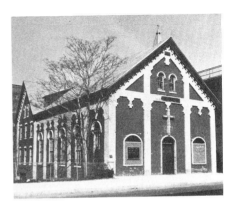

The Mission Chapel
131-C

The Mission Chapel (today the Second Baptist Church) is one of the oldest church buildings in Worcester. It boasts a variety of historical associations. Concerned that the Evangelical City Missionary Society, formed in 1849 and joined later by other Protestant churches, should have a City Mission Chapel "to give the poor and neglected a place of worship free," Ichabod Washburn, a deacon of the Missionary Society designed and built the chapel for $14,000 in 1854. The building contained a chapel, living quarters for the city missionary, and space for the Mission's Pine Meadow Sunday school. Partially restored in 1966 when the building was returned to religious use as a Baptist Church, the Mission Chapel bears elements of the Norman style Romanesque popular around 1845 to 1875. Characteristic are its recessed wall panels and decorative brickwork. In the 1860s, the Mission had its greatest growth under Henry T. Cheever. With Washburn's help, he began an industrial school "to give instruction in sewing . . . The average number enjoying these advantages is two hundred fifty, mostly Irish Catholics." Later in the century, the chapel was used by German, Swedish, Armenian, and French congregations before each became sufficiently established to build a church of its own.

St. John Catholic Church
40 Temple Street
P. W. Ford

St. John Catholic Church
131-K

St. John Catholic Church is the oldest church building in Worcester (1845), and the city's only example of Greek Revival church architecture. Built of brick, the church rises from a granite plinth to a low-pitched roof. The building's facade is symmetrical, containing a projecting central pavilion framed by paired pilasters which support a pediment. Above the pavilion is a square-plan tower which rises to a wooden belfry and spire. While the belfry may be original, the present spire dates from the 1940s. Flanking the central pavilion are single entries surmounted by arched windows. Access to the facade's three entries is gained by three separate flights of granite stairs. Side walls of the church are divided into bays of equal size by paired brick piers; each bay contains a single arched window.

Worcester's oldest Catholic parish, St. John traces its origins to 1834 when the Reverend James Fitton was designated by Bishop Fenwick to visit Worcester once each month to conduct religious services for the town's 80 Catholics. In the same year Father Fitton tried to buy a lot at the corner of Salem and Park Streets where he intended to build a church. According to local tradition, the lot's sellers learned of its intended use and as a result destroyed the deed, refusing to carry out the sale. In July 1834, part of the present Temple Street property was purchased by several Worcester natives who then transferred title to Father Fitton. Foundations for a wooden church were laid and the building completed in 1835. Local histories report that this first building was constructed by Irish laborers, most of whom had come to Worcester to work for the railroad. During the 1840s increasing Irish immigration brought several thousand immigrants to Worcester, causing St. John to outgrow its first church. In 1845 the old church was moved and the present church was built on the newly cleared site. By June 1846, the present church with a planned capacity of 1,450 people was completed, appearing much as it does today.

Main Street Baptist Church
717 Main Street

Main Street Baptist Church
142-E

The Third Baptist Church, known as the Main Street Baptist Church after 1864, was constructed in two stages: the rear chapel in 1853, the main church in 1855. Designed in what was then called the "Norman style of architecture," the church is the city's only remaining example of this style which enjoyed limited popularity in the mid-nineteenth century. Although this "Norman" style was derived from Romanesque sources, it is a completely separate style from Romanesque Revival style which was popularized under the influence of H. H. Richardson in the last quarter of the nineteenth century. Characteristic of this early and fanciful taste for Romanesque architecture are the building's recessed wall panels, buttresses, corbelling, and recessed arched entry with bands of geometric ornament. The main church was dedicated on January 9, 1856 at a service conducted by the church's pastor, H. L. Wayland and his father, Dr. Wayland, president of Brown University.

The Third Baptist Society was formed in 1852 when Eli Thayer, a prominent educator, businessman and politician, led an off-shoot group of the First Baptist Church. The congregation first met in the old City Hall, later in Brinley Hall, and, in 1853, in the chapel at the rear of the present building. Among other activities, the congregation was active in its support of Worcester Academy and in the establishment of a French Baptist chapel on Beacon Street. By 1902 the congregation had rejoined the First Baptist Church and the Main Street church became the property of the First Presbyterian Church of Worcester. In recent years it has come back under the Baptist umbrella and is now the Emmanuel Baptist Church.

St. Peter's Catholic Church
152-C

St. Peter's Catholic Church
935 Main Street
P. W. Ford (Boston)

In May of 1884, St. Peter's Catholic Church was formed to provide a separate church for the growing Catholic population of Worcester's southwestern sections, particularly in the vicinity of Main Street south. Reverend Daniel H. O'Neill was appointed to form the parish and, on June 6, 1884, ground was broken for the present building. On September 7, 1884, the church's cornerstone was laid and the congregation began using the basement chapel late in 1884, although the church was not fully completed until 1893.

Designed by P. W. Ford of Boston, who designed many of Worcester's Roman Catholic churches, St. Peter's Catholic Church is predominantly Victorian Gothic style and is one of Worcester's most ornate Victorian church buildings. The building is built of red brick with granite trim. The church plan consists of a high nave with enclosed side aisles, transept and square-plan tower at the nave's southwest corner. The church's facade contains three entries set in arches with alternating brick and stone voussoirs. Above are oculi with quatrifoliate tracery (side aisles) and three arches containing paired windows and decorative brick panels. Over these is a rose window. The tower rises in stages with buttresses at the corners of its first two stories. At the tower's third storey is a belfry framed by paired arches on each wall. Above the belfry is a corbelled cornice, crenellated parapet, and pinnacles.

South Unitarian Church
886 Main Street
Earle & Fisher

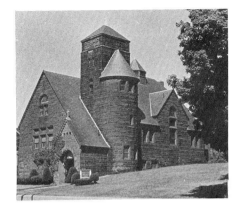

South Unitarian Church
153-C

Built in 1894, the former South Unitarian Church is an unusual example of Romanesque Revival style with an asymmetrical plan and complex roof. Exterior walls are of rock-faced sandstone, laid up in courses of regularly alternating widths. The building's facade contains a high gable with tripartite windows and an arched window providing light to the church hall. At the building's northeast corner is an arched entry set in a gabled porch behind which is a square-plan tower and semi-circular side tower. Both north and south elevations bear the same high quality stonework as the facade. Alterations are restricted to the repointing of a small portion of the tower and the removal of a belfry.

The South Unitarian Society was established in 1890, partly through the efforts of Reverend Austin Garver, pastor of the First Unitarian Church (Second Parish) of Worcester. The congregation's first minister was George W. Kent. Early meetings of the society were held at the Freeland Street Schoolhouse, at Pilgrim Church Hall, and finally in a storefront on Main Street, opposite 886 Main Street. Early in 1894 the congregation commissioned plans for a church from Earle & Fisher, architects. Construction apparently took place the same year.

The South Unitarian Society formed to "provide for the needs of those living in the southern part" of the city, was one of more than a half dozen new congregations organized during the 1880s and 1890s as a result of the growth in population of the Main Street South area. Of the other congregations formed at this time, the Pilgrim Congregational Church and St. Mark's Episcopal Church also built Romanesque Revival style churches designed by Earle & Fisher. Constructed by the Norcross Brothers, the South Unitarian Church is a fine and very well-preserved example of this style.

At one time this church belonged to the Springfield Catholic Diocese and was used as a parish hall by St. Peter's Church in the 1940s. It was purchased by and became the Armenian National Apostolic Holy Trinity Church in 1948. The church changed hands again in 1980 when bought by the Seventh Day Adventist Church.

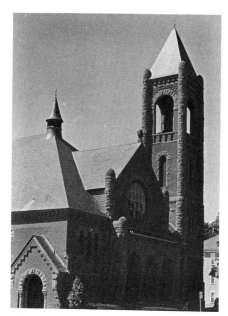

Pilgrim Congregational Church
153-E

Pilgrim Congregational Church
909 Main Street
Stephen C. Earle

The Pilgrim Congregational Church is an unusual example of Romanesque Revival architecture. Designed by Stephen Earle, the building is constructed of brick with rock-faced sandstone window and corner trim. Nearly rectangular in plan, the church has gables on its facade and side walls, apparently corresponding to the nave and transept. Principal features of the building are a high corner tower which rises to an open belfry and is trimmed with rounded stone corners and spiral-carved stone finials, a tripartite arched entry porch, rose window and arched windows throughout. Both the high quality of the building's design and its excellent condition make it an unusually fine example of Victorian architecture.

Organized in May 1883, the Pilgrim Congregational Church was "received into the Congregational fellowship" in March of 1885. Land at the corner of Main and Gardner Streets had been given to the congregation by Francis B. Knowles and Mrs. Helen C. Knowles. A wooden chapel had been built on the property in 1884 and was first occupied in January of 1885. In 1886 an effort was made to collect donations for the construction of a more substantial building. As a result, the cornerstone of the present church was laid on October 22, 1887. Constructed by the building firm of Cutting & Bishop, the church was completed by July 1888. Around the same time the wooden chapel was remodeled for use as a Sunday school.

St. Mark's Episcopal Church
Freeland Street
Stephen C. Earle

St. Mark's Episcopal Church
164-G

Designed by Stephen C. Earle and built, it is believed, by the Norcross Brothers in 1888, St. Mark's is an especially fine and unusual example of Romanesque Revival style. Constructed of rock-faced sandstone laid in a broken course, the building consists of two rectangular plan sections set perpendicularly to each other. The front section has an asymmetrical facade with virtually no decoration save for the deep voussoirs (one of the wedge-shaped pieces forming an arch) and two carved medallions on either side of the entry arch. Fenestration of the facade is irregular, perhaps reflecting interior arrangements and the desire to achieve picturesque asymmetry. The front section is approximately one and one half storeys high and contains the parish house. The rear section houses a chapel capable of seating 350 people. All of the elevations are largely unornamented leaving the beautiful stonework as the chief decorative element in its design.

St. Mark's was formed as a mission in 1887 and officially recognized as a parish in 1888. The church building was dedicated on February 7, 1889. It was the third of four Episcopal mission churches founded in Worcester through the encouragement of the Reverend William Huntington, rector of All Saints (the city's only Episcopal church until 1883). According to Huntington's concept, the four new congregations formed between 1883 and 1903 were named for the first four evangelists: Matthew, Mark, Luke and John.

St. Matthew's Episcopal Church
165-H

St. Matthew's Episcopal Church
699 Southbridge Street
Stephen C. Earle

Constructed of rock-faced granite and ornamented with Gothic and Romanesque motifs, St. Matthew's Church was constructed by the Norcross Brothers and remains in original condition. The building's Southbridge facade consists of the high gable of the nave (with rose window) beneath which is a slight porch with pointed-arch entry. North of the nave is a square-plan tower which rises in stages to a belfry, crenellated parapet and low, pyramidal roof. At the tower's northwest corner is a circular-plan side tower which rises to a conical (stone roof) and finial. Side elevations of the church have side aisles of stone construction above which are stucco-covered clerestories. Immediately south of the church and connected to it by a passageway is a modern parish house.

St. Matthew's was the first of four Episcopal missions to be founded in Worcester through the encouragement of William Huntington, rector of All Saints Episcopal Church from 1862 to 1883, later rector of Grace Church in New York City. Named for the writers of the four Gospels, these missions were founded between 1869 and 1908. Money began to be raised for St. Matthew's in 1869. Land was purchased at the corner of Southbridge and Washburn Streets where a wooden chapel was built in 1871. In 1874 the mission was reorganized as a parish with Henry MacKay as the first rector. By 1880 when the first church was consecrated, the parish had fifty members. In 1882 additional land was purchased and a hall constructed.

Movement to construct the present building began in 1890 with the purchase of its lot. A rectory was built in 1890, but the church was not begun until 1893. The cornerstone was set in May of 1894 at a ceremony attended by Bishop William Lawrence who also consecrated the building on May 22, 1896.

All major windows were made by Tiffany & Company.

CHAPTER VIII
HOUSES Pre-1830

*See National Landmarks, page 15

photo on page 129
Salisbury Mansion

Nineteenth century local historians reported that the early settlers lived in log huts and dug-out dwellings for a number of years after arrival. This tradition notwithstanding, it seems unlikely that early settlers lived in such crude structures, particularly as both the second and third settlement companies included at least three house wrights out of a total of 36 men in 1684, and at least thirteen in 1713–1717. Further, the early establishment of sawmills would have provided the most important materials for construction of timber-frame houses like those the settlers knew in their native coastal towns. None of the early houses located along Main Street remain. However, some former farmhouses remain in scattered locations, such as the Benjamin Flagg House, the Chamberlain-Flagg House and the William McFarland House. All of these display the regional taste for central chimney houses with symmetrical facades containing only three openings instead of the more popular five-opening facade found in other parts of the state. Another regional type, the distinguishing feature of which is a chimney passing through the center of a hip roof, is typified by the Smith-Thaxter-Merrifield House. The social homogeneity of the original farming community is reflected in these largely undecorated houses; however, with the gradual emergence of a mercantile and court-based gentry, Georgian decorative details began to appear on the homes of the town's leading citizens such as the Paine House (The Oaks) and the Stephen Salisbury Mansion.

As with the Georgian houses that once stood along Main Street, Federalist domestic architecture achieved its most elaborate forms along Main Street between the Common and Lincoln Square. Almost completely obliterated, this style is now best represented by additions made to the Salisbury Mansion in 1818. Simpler examples of the style may be seen in the Stearns Tavern and the Chadwick Brittan House.

Smith-Thaxter-Merrifield House
158 Holden Street

Smith-Thaxter-Merrifield House
24-C

Known locally as the Merrifield House, ca. 1741, this is among Worcester's oldest and is an excellent example of eighteenth century vernacular architecture. Of timber-frame construction, the house has a nearly square floor plan with a massive central chimney rising through the center of the structure's hip roof. The facade is symmetrical consisting of a center entry flanked on each side by two windows on the first storey and five windows on the second. The facade entry has an elaborate twelve-panel door set between thin pilasters which support a dentilled cap. Once a common building type in Worcester, central chimney hip-roofed houses are now very rare. There are only three examples extant: the old section of the Salisbury Mansion, the Nathan White House at 920 Southbridge Street, and the Merrifield House. In its present form, Merrifield may be the product of a late eighteenth century renovation in which the original structure was enlarged and both the hip roof and front entry added. More recent additions are limited to the replacement of the original sash, perhaps in the early twentieth century.

The first owner was probably Elisha Smith II, a native of Weston who settled in Worcester near North Pond before the birth of his daughter, Mary, in 1741. Between 1775 and 1792 the house was sold to Benjamin Thaxter who occupied it until early in the next century. According to an 1890 history by Caleb Wall, the house was purchased by Deacon Alpheus Merrifield about 1849 for his son Francis, who operated a farm there. In 1866 the farm and house were bought by James Libby whose heirs owned the property until 1915 when it was sold to Norton Company which, in 1946, presented this 12-room house to the Worcester Children's Friend Society.

Amos Flagg House
44-C

Amos Flagg House
246 Burncoat Street

Located north of the center of Worcester, in an area which was rural until World War I, the Amos Flagg House is one of the city's few well preserved timber-frame houses. Consisting of a one storey rear ell, the front section has a central chimney, asymmetrical facade (one door and three windows), 12/12 and 8/12 sash, and a sunken four-panel front door (ca. 1790-1820) surmounted by a four-pane transom. The house appears unaltered after 1820.

Of apparent eighteenth century origin, the Amos Flagg House has a murky history. It is not noted on Caleb Wall's "Map of Worcester's Earliest Settlers" published in 1877. During most of the nineteenth century the house belonged to Jonathan White, a farmer. White is thought to have come to Worcester in 1801 and worked on the farm of Joel Gleason, later on the farm of Amos Flagg, who had married Betsey Gleason, daughter of Joel. After Flagg's death in 1825, White married Flagg's widow and took title to the property. Until 1914 the house and farm remained in the possession of White's heirs. After 1914, the surrounding area was subdivided into house lots and the Amos Flagg House was sold to Frederick Nelson who retained ownership into the 1970s.

It seems most likely that the house was constructed for Alan (Allen) Flagg on a fifty-acre parcel which Flagg sold (or perhaps mortgaged) to Jonas Gale of Waltham in 1748. During the eighteenth century the property (with alterations in its boundaries) changed hands several times within the Gleason and Flagg families. Owned briefly by Silas and Amos Flagg jointly in 1807, the house was not owned solely by Amos Flagg until 1816, the year of his marriage. Although the Flagg House is among the best preserved "Cape Cod" style houses in Worcester, it has been largely unnoticed by the traditional sources of historical information.

William McFarland House
525 Salisbury Street

William McFarland House
63-B

Best estimates of the construction of this farm house fall between 1743 and 1759. It was built for William McFarland (1722-1805) on land given to him by his father, Andrew. There were several early McFarland houses in this area of Worcester, so it is difficult to be certain just which belonged to William McFarland, Sr. who later became a lieutenant in the Revolution. It is almost certain that his son, William, Jr. (1758-1839) owned this house. And there is no doubt that 525 Salisbury Street is one of Worcester's finest and best preserved eighteenth century "Cape Cod" type structures.

In the early nineteenth century McFarland, Jr. married Anna Davis. Sometime in the 1830s the McFarlands deeded the house to their daughter, Sarah Gale, wife of Cyrus Gale, retaining life estate for themselves. After the deaths of Anna and Sarah, the property was sold in 1858 to George T. Foster, a farmer, who occupied it through the remainder of the century. Part of the uncertainty in determining the house's origin comes from varying references as to whether or not the house of William, Sr. was on the east side of Salisbury Street. Whether or not 525 Salisbury Street was constructed at the earlier or later range of dates given, it is a rare survivor of Worcester's earlier, rural development.

Characteristic of vernacular architecture in the vicinity of Worcester, the McFarland House is a rectangular plan building with a central chimney and rear ell. The house is set on a rubble-stone foundation and is enclosed by a pitched roof. The wide spacing of the facade's three openings (two windows and a central entry) has strong associations with buildings dating from the early eighteenth century settlement of Worcester County.

Chadwick-Brittan House
309 Lincoln Street

Chadwick-Brittan House
66-D

Built about 1797, the Chadwick-Brittan House is among Worcester's few well preserved houses of the Federalist period. Checkered and confusing in its background, the house was known during the mid-nineteenth century as the home of Josiah Brittan who owned sizeable tracts of land around Adams Square on both the east and west sides of Lincoln Street, parts of which were occupied by his brickyard. After Brittan's death, the property passed into the possession of his wife, followed by George H. Lane, a blacksmith, and later Josiah Shattuck, owner of the Worcester Truck Company. During the late 1880s and 1890s the property was subdivided and developed with cottages and Queen Anne style houses. It is possible that the Chadwick-Brittan House has been moved slightly on its original lot to make way for Shaffner Street.

The earlier history of the house is less clear. According to Caleb Wall's "Map of Earliest Settlers" (pub. 1877), two hotels existed in Adams Square in the early nineteenth century, the Chadwick Hotel (opened around 1800) and the Leonard Clark Hotel (opened around 1824). Of these two, the Chadwick Hotel occupied a site closer to that of 309 Lincoln Street. A 1931 account of the house states that it was built around 1797 and that it was used as the Chadwick Tavern. Other sources give the same (1797) date, referring to the building as "Lydia Chadwick's Inn." By 1833, the building had ceased to be used as an inn and was owned by an A. D. Foster.

The house's brick foundation, 6/9 sash, center entrance with Greek Revival frame, and twin interior chimneys all survive. Porches and dormers may have been added in the early 1900s.

Chamberlain-Flagg House
2 Brookshire Road

Chamberlain-Flagg House
74-A

Another of Worcester's oldest, the Chamberlain-Flagg House has an unclear history. The house consists of a rectangular-plan main structure with a central chimney and a two storey wing on the west wall of the main building. The facade is nearly symmetrical with a center entrance flanked by one 12/12 window on either side at the first storey with three more 12/12 in the second storey. This facade arrangement resembles many houses in Worcester and the surrounding area which have historical associations with the early eighteenth century—the area's first period of permanent settlement. The location of the present structure was the product of one or more early additions. Details, such as the Colonial Revival style entry, side porches, and an exterior chimney were added in the early twentieth century.

Although most sources refer to the building as the Flagg House, it is identified in Nutt's *History of Worcester* as the Chamberlain House. As this area of the city was settled by Jacob Chamberlain and his descendants (on land purchased partly from Richard Flagg) after 1742, it is likely that the house's earliest associations are with the Chamberlain family. Marked as the house of Elisha Flagg from 1800 (map of earliest settlers) through 1851, the house may have come into possession of the Flagg family through Flagg's wife, a daughter of William Chamberlain. Until 1930 the house remained in the Flagg family and was renowned for the family's live peacocks. In 1930 the property and thirty-seven acres of land were sold to a real estate developer who had intended to demolish the house. Happily, the house was sold instead with a large lot, and remains intact as a residence. The antiquity of the structure, and its well preserved interior, mark it as one of the best remaining eighteenth century houses in Worcester.

Timothy Paine House
90-C

Timothy Paine House (The Oaks)
140 Lincoln Street

Built between 1774 and 1778, The Oaks stands out from its neighbors as the oldest in the vicinity and, indeed, it is one of the oldest surviving structures in Worcester. The house is set back from the road approximately one hundred feet and has a circular drive in front.

The Oaks is two and one half storeys covered with clapboards painted red with white trim. Although the east side faces Lincoln Street, the original entrance was on the south side of the house. The entrance consists of a two storey projecting section. The doorway is flanked by pilasters topped with a pediment and above the door on the second storey is a window. The south facade is five bays wide and the shuttered windows have 6/6 sash. Two dormers with paired windows (2/2 sash) extend from the ridge roof, and a brick chimney is situated between them.

At a later date the entrance was changed to the east side of the house. Positioned slightly off center, the doorway has an elliptical fanlight and sidelights. Windows on this facade also have 6/6 sash and are topped by projecting caps. The two windows to the right of the door differ slightly by being floor-length. The east side extends an additional bay to the north because of an ell on that end. The one storey porch, added when the doorway was changed, stretches the length of the east facade. A handsome balustrade tops this porch which is supported by four slender Doric columns.

In 1836 another addition was made. This was the kitchen ell which extends from the northwest corner of the house. Fenestration on this wing corresponds to that of the earlier portion of the house. It is said that at the time of this addition, a soldier's hat was found in the partitions, thus substantiating the claim that Revolutionary War soldiers had been quartered in the house.

The Oaks, or the Paine House, is significant because of its association with the Tory Judge, Timothy Paine and with the well-known descendants of the Paine family.

Judge Timothy Paine was born in Bristol, Rhode Island and came to Worcester when he was nine years old. By 1751 Paine was dealing in real estate. In 1767 he purchased three hundred acres of land on the "great road to Boston," now known as Lincoln Street. This tract later became known as the North End and included what is now Rural Cemetery. Running from the Salisbury estate on the west to the Green estate on the east, the area contains many streets which bear names in the Paine family tree.

Timothy Paine married the daughter of Judge Chandler, and in 1774 he began his estate on Lincoln Street. Because of his Tory leanings and the resulting hostility shown him by the local community, work on the house was not completed until 1778.

The Oaks remained in the Paine family until 1914 when it was sold to the Daughters of the American Revolution. It is now the headquarters of the Colonel Timothy Bigelow chapter of the D.A.R.

The Salisbury Mansion and Store
40 Highland Street
Abraham Savage (Boston)

The Salisbury Mansion and Store are significant to the City of Worcester because of their long association with the Salisbury family who were prominent in Worcester's commercial activity and important contributors to Worcester's cultural heritage. The buildings also have great architectural significance. The Mansion is one of the oldest, and certainly the grandest extant house from its period, and the Store is an excellent example of provincial classical architecture.

The Mansion was built in 1772 for Stephen Salisbury I, by Dean Joseph Allen of Hardwick from designs submitted by Abraham Savage. The house was originally constructed in Lincoln Square. Stephen I, moved to Worcester in 1767 at the age of twenty-one to establish a hardware store in partnership with his brother, Samuel, of Boston. The store was first located in a small rented building, but when the Mansion was erected the store occupied part of the first floor. In 1790, the building now called the Salisbury Store was built on the property, and served as a warehouse. The actual shop remained in the Mansion until 1818, when Samuel Salisbury's death brought an end to the partnership. That year the shop was moved

The Salisbury Mansion
102-O

The Salisbury Store
102-O

into the Store, and the space it vacated in the Mansion was turned into two parlors.

Various interior and exterior alterations were made until 1819 when, with the addition of the delicate Classical Revival portico, the house took on the appearance it has today. Both the Mansion and Store were moved in 1929 to their present locations to prevent their destruction.

The Mansion is two storeys high with a hip roof and irregular window spacing on the facade. A pedimented center gable with modillions and an oculus emphasizes the one storey portico beneath it. The portico is supported by five slender Corinthian columns and is topped by a balustrade. The windows are all 6/6, and each one is topped by a cornice with modillions. Wooden quoins delineate the corners of the house and modillions support the cornice. There are four irregularly placed chimneys and the main door, with an elliptical fan light and long narrow side lights flanked by slender pilasters, is off center under the portico.

The interior of the Mansion contains most of its original eighteenth century woodwork. The wainscoting and window trim are characteristic of the third quarter of the eighteenth century. The interior pilasters, paneling, door frames and cornices, with their elegant but restrained regularity, also seem to date from the original construction of the house. The two east drawing rooms, decorated when the store was finally removed in 1819, have woodwork characteristic of this period, with a few details probably added in the 1830s.

The Salisbury Store was constructed next to the Salisbury Mansion in 1790 for use as a storeroom. After the Store was moved, it was restored to its original condition based on elevation drawings found in the Salisbury Papers. It is two storeys high with a hip roof. In the center of the roof, a small square enclosed structure houses the original hoist, and the interior loft remains intact. There are four 9/6 windows with plain trim on the first floor of the facade and a modern shed porch. The second floor has two non-original 12/12 windows on either side of a central Palladian window, and each end elevation contains an oculus on the second floor. Thin boarding laid on top of the clapboards divide the Store into arched bays, three on the facade and one on each of the end elevations.

The Mansion is now owned by the Salisbury Associates and is operated by the Worcester Historical Museum as a house museum. The Store is owned by the Bay State Society for the Crippled and Handicapped and used for their offices.

Benjamin Flagg House
136 Plantation Street

One of the oldest houses in Worcester is the Benjamin Flagg homestead at 136 Plantation Street thought to have been built about 1717. With the locally popular central chimney, center entrance, and narrow three-window facade, this farmhouse is typical of the style erected by the city's earliest settlers. Benjamin Flagg II (son of Benjamin Flagg I of Watertown, later of Auburn) was born in Watertown in 1691. About 1717 he bought large tracts of land in Worcester. A carpenter by trade, he is believed to have built the house around this time. Flagg, a man of many parts, was a selectman in 1729, served as local schoolmaster and, in 1751, as sheriff of the county. Benjamin Flagg III, whose name is most often associated with the house, was born in Worcester in 1724, served in the French and Indian War, and marched with Colonel Timothy Bigelow's company of Minute Men in April 1775. He died in 1818 leaving 4 children, 42 grandchildren, and 83 great grandchildren.

Recently restored, the Flagg house now appears as it does in nineteenth century photographs except for the addition of a Colonial Revival front door and a large multi-paned window on the south side.

Benjamin Flagg House
132-A

Stearns Tavern
651 Park Avenue

Now a branch office of Home Federal Savings and Loan Association, the old Stearns Tavern was originally located at 1030 Main Street prior to the 1974 move to 651 Park Avenue. Previously it had been an antique shop, a furniture shop, and the Harrington House of Carpets. Although it is not known when the building was built, it is possible the framing dates from the mid-eighteenth century but unlikely any of the structure's exterior pre-dates 1812—the year the tavern was opened by Charles Stearns. After brief ownership, Stearns sold out to Dean Uriah Stone who kept it only a few years. Between 1824-1830, the tavern was operated as a hotel by Joseph Curtis who sold the property to C. M. Delant about 1837.

It is a two storey timber-frame house with a symmetrical center entrance

Stearns Tavern
163-C

facade and twin chimneys. Located at the building's northeast corner is a two storey wing housing the present bank hall. The main entry contains an unusual six-panel door set between sidelights surmounted by a low fanlight. Side entries to the main house are set in molded architraves capped by entablatures and cornices. At the time of the move an enclosed, one bay entry porch was removed from the facade to reveal the present doorway. The building is thought to be Worcester's best example of Federalist Vernacular architecture.

CHAPTER IX
HOUSES &
APARTMENTS
Post-1830

HOUSES AND APARTMENTS Post-1830

With the population explosion that accompanied industrialization, new neighborhoods were laid out on the hillsides surrounding the Mill Brook and Main Street. The most ambitious of these new neighborhoods were the Oxford-Crown Hill District and the area around Grant Square (Windsor and Catherine Streets) which were laid out into house lots around small parks. These parks were mostly eliminated during the initial sale of lots. Another popular neighborhood was developed by Levi Lincoln, Jr. who first subdivided the Sever Farm (Chestnut and Elm Streets) and later his own estate north of Elm Street. North of the Lincoln Estate, Harvard Street was laid out on Court Hill in the 1840s and quickly became built up with Greek Revival and Italianate houses and with some Gothic Revival cottages. East of Main Street, Chandler Hill (Earle, Elizabeth, Prospect, Mulberry, Laurel and other streets) began to be developed as small properties were opened up piecemeal. Near Main Street South (Ionic Avenue, Sycamore, Charlton and Beacon Streets) land formerly owned by Worcester Academy was auctioned off as houselots, although only limited development took place here before the early 1860s.

These new neighborhoods were defined clearly by class and use, partly through the work of Elias Carter, a housewright and architect who gave architectural expression to growing class distinctions. Along Main Street by the Common and along Chestnut and Elm Streets, Carter designed a large number of two-story, hip-roofed Greek Revival style houses, most with two story porticos. Built at first for the city's gentry in the 1830s, houses of this type rapidly became popular for wealthy merchants and manufacturers, providing a plan and type which lingered on in local Italianate architecture. To a lesser degree, temple-front houses enjoyed a brief popularity.

More widespread and by far the most popular house type of the period were the two storey side hall plan Greek Revival style houses with pedimented gables, and other simple Greek Revival style trim. While the

photo on page 141
Aldus Higgins House

earliest known example of this type was designed by Elias Carter as a temporary home for Governor Levi Lincoln during the construction of his Elm Street mansion, most houses of this type appear to have been designed by builders. Characteristics of this type house were corner pilasters, pedimented gables, entablature/cornices, and Doric porches.

Also popular at this time were Carpenter Gothic cottages. The most well preserved examples of the style are the Bentley-Jackson Cottage and slightly later, Soho and Forest Hills Cottages. Introduced in the early 1850s and remaining popular into the 1860s, Italianate architecture was once widespread throughout the city but now remains only in a few examples. Of the many stucco covered villas designed by Elbridge Boyden and built on hillside estates, none remain. Slightly less elaborate, wood frame villas remain on former rural sites. The broader influence of the Italianate style can be seen throughout the city in the many side-hall plan houses bearing Italianate brackets and trim.

In keeping with a brief national taste for octagonal houses, two such were built in Worcester: the Elias Crawford House and the Barker House; the latter of which is built of stone chips and mortar in the manner of Orson Squire Fowler's gravel-wall construction.

The Second Empire style made its first appearance in Worcester in the 1850s. Early examples share the same plan, symmetrical facades, concavely curved mansard roofs and other decorative details many of which display the lingering influence of the Italianate style. Later examples, built during the 1870s make use of straight sided mansards, asymmetrical plans and more geometric neo-Grec ornament.

Co-existing with Second Empire style architecture, the local taste for the Victorian Gothic style began in the late 1860s. Although a few were built of brick, a number of extremely ornate, wood frame houses were built in this style. They exhibit exceptional porches, bargeboards, aprons and window trim, all decorated with quatrefoils, trefoils, pointed arches, and other Gothic motifs.

The construction of the Norcross Brothers Houses in 1879 marked the beginning of local Queen Anne style architecture. Built during a 30-year period, the Queen Anne style is one of the most widely represented architectural styles in Worcester. Likely to have been designed by the Norcross Brothers themselves, their houses were far in advance of local taste. Their effect on local architects is apparent in the large number of Queen Anne houses of 1880–1884 which are modelled on the plan of the Norcross Houses. After an initial period of experimentation, local architects seem to have favored wood frame construction, corner towers, and decorative shingling for subsequent designs in this style.

Beginning in the late 1870s, apartment houses began to be built around Lincoln Square, Pleasant Street, Chandler Street and along Main Street (south) and particularly in the vicinity of Wellington Street. The most widespread building type of this period, and of the subsequent period to 1930, was the "three decker," a three storey structure containing three apartments, generally of the same floor plan. The low cost of this type of housing along with a large amount of air and light made it an attractive form of working class housing, particularly for the city's immigrants.

The period of 1891–1917 saw a doubling of local population. As areas in the southern and eastern sections of the city became built up with three deckers, single family homes dominated the development of the west side. The lingering popularity of Queen Anne architecture in these areas did not prevent a stylistic explosion which saw local architects designing elaborate neo-Tudor houses and Colonial Revival style houses. More eclectic styles became popular in the early twentieth century with houses bearing evidence of the Arts and Crafts movement, Prairie style and Bungalow style throughout the west side.

Ezra Rice House (1833–1845)
1133 West Boylston Street

Bearing a close resemblance to the Charles Newton House at 24 Brattle Street, the Ezra Rice House is an early example of Greek Revival architecture, and one which retains elements of the Federalist style. The house is a two storey frame structure set on a foundation of rock-faced granite. The facade is three bays wide trimmed with narrow corner boards and a pedimented gable. The entry, nearly identical to that of the Newton House, is one of two of its type in Worcester. Derived from patterns published in Asher Benjamin's builders companions of the 1830s, the doorway contains an original panelled door flanked by side lights and surrounded by an architrave with decorative center and corner blocks. Alterations to the house are minor, consisting of the enclosure of a rear porch.

The Rice House is not listed in local directories until 1851 when it was occupied by Ezra Beaman Rice (1825–1912), a farmer. Little is known of Rice, who occupied the house until his death, although his name suggests that he was a grandson of Ezra Beaman. The elder Beaman was a prominent citizen of Boylston and West Boylston who fought as a major in the Revolution and later served as a representative to the General Court. The Beaman family's long-standing ties to West Boylston and the distance of the house from the center of Worcester probably account for the scant information regarding Ezra Beaman Rice.

Charles Newton House (1833–1845)
24 Brattle Street

An early example of the popular side-hall type of Greek Revival style house, the Charles Newton House is a two and one half storey frame structure set on a foundation of rock-faced granite. Although the building's pedimented facade is characteristically Greek Revival, some elements, such as its narrow corner boards, window trim and narrow cornice are holdovers from Federalist architecture. Particularly fine and rare in Worcester is the house's entry consisting of an original six-panel door set between side lights and surrounded by an architrave with corner

Ezra Rice House
4-A

Charles Newton House
17-C

and center blocks. Derived from patterns published in Asher Benjamin's builders companions of the 1830s, this doorway is one of two of its type existent in Worcester (the other can be found on the Ezra Rice House).

Located north of the city's center, the Newton House is in an area which was not listed in Worcester directories until the 1850s when the house was occupied by Charles Newton, a farmer. Later, the house was owned by Calvin Foster, a hardware dealer and president of the City National Bank of Worcester. In 1890, Foster rented and later sold the house to James Fuller, a partner in the locally prominent architecture firm of Fuller and Delano. Fuller (1836–1901), a native of Warwick, Massachusetts, practiced architecture in Worcester from 1867 to 1901. Between 1867 and 1876, Fuller was a member of the firm of Earle and Fuller. In 1879, Fuller entered into partnership with Ward Delano (Fuller & Delano) with whom he designed many well-known buildings, including the Worcester State Armory, the Chase Building, part of the campus of Worcester Academy, and the Old South Church built in 1888. After Fuller's death, the firm continued as Fuller and Delano Company under the direction of Fuller's son, Robert, who also lived at 24 Brattle Street in the first decades of the twentieth century.

John Brooks House (ca. 1850)
12 Nelson Place

John Brooks (1809–1894), a native of Princeton, came to Worcester in 1837. By 1847 he had purchased a farm called the "Nelson Place" on which he may have built the west wing of the present house, a smaller cottage, as a building is shown in this approximate location on the 1851 map of Worcester. According to Brooks' obituary, the present house was built in 1856 and remained his home until 1881. Brooks was a deacon of Central Church from 1863 to 1879; a member of the Massachusetts State Legislature in 1854, 1885 and 1886; a member of the Worcester Common Council in 1850–1851. In addition to farming, Brooks worked as a blacksmith and was involved in real estate development in the Chadwick Square and Greendale sections of the city. The property remains in the possession of Brooks' descendants.

John Brooks House
53-A

The Brooks House is a one and one half storey frame house, built to give the appearance of a cottage. The facade is three bays wide at the first storey, rising to a steep gable with an oculus at the attic. At the first storey, the facade has a side hall entry, two oversized windows, and a full porch with open supports and original brackets. Unusual for buildings of this type, the Brooks House has three bracketed gables on the side elevation. On the west wall is a rectangular plan ell set at right angles to the main body of the house. Alterations have been minor, consisting of a one storey frame addition to the north end of the east elevation. In its present condition, the Brooks House is a particularly fine example of locally popular cottage type of the 1850s and 1860s.

George Gabriel House (1899)
31 Lenox Street

Built as part of the McFarland-Chamberlain Farm which was subdivided to create Richmond Heights around 1896, the Gabriel House is a fine example of Colonial Revival architecture. The rectangular plan, hip roof, Ionic Pilasters, and dormers are characteristic elements of Colonial Revival design. Other, less usual features include a second storey bowed oriel with Palladian window, splayed window lintels with keystones, and Ionic porches with original balustrades. Currently in excellent condition, the Gabriel House stands out as one of the earliest and finest houses in the Richmond Heights area.

The first occupant of this dwelling was George Gabriel, a bookkeeper and later manager of the George Blake Company, dealers in iron, steel and other metals. Gabriel's move here in 1899, from a house at 8 Melville Street which he had built in 1891, is characteristic of the change in residential patterns which occurred in the nineteenth and early twentieth centuries. Earlier, Victorian middle and upper-class areas had existed on all sides of the center city. By the 1880s, districts north, east and south of the business district were being by-passed in favor of the city's west side, particularly such areas as the former Lincoln Estate and Elm Park district, Hammond Heights, and later Richmond Heights.

George Gabriel House
86-B

Harry Goddard House
89-B

Harry Goddard House (1905)
190 Salisbury Street

George Clemence

The Goddard House is a two and one half storey frame house with a hip roof. The symmetrical facade has two sets of semi-circular bay windows, a center entrance, and Palladian window over the entry. Named "Elmarion," the front section of the house is unaltered. Designed by George Clemence and built in 1905, it was described and illustrated upon its completion in an article in *The Worcester Magazine*. In 1915 the rear wing was partially rebuilt creating, on its south elevation, an entry set behind a semi-circular porch, and three sets of glazed French doors with decorative railings (second storey), all of which changed the orientation of the house from Park Avenue to Salisbury Street. Located at the outer edge of the Massachusetts Avenue Historic District, the Goddard House is of similar architectural quality of buildings in the district and shares similar historical associations.

The first owner of the house was Harry Goddard (1863–1927), one of the city's most prominent manufacturers at the turn of the century. Goddard, a native of Holyoke, Massachusetts, entered the employ of the Spencer Wire Company at the age of seventeen. Around 1884, at the age of twenty-one, Goddard was made superintendent of the company's mill. In 1895, upon the death of the company's owner, Goddard purchased a controlling interest in the firm and became the company's president and general manager. By 1900, the growth of the company under Goddard's direction had resulted in the construction of a new plant at the junction of Webster and Jacques Streets. By 1917, approximately eight hundred people were employed in the Webster Street plant. In addition to interests in several other businesses, Goddard was elected president of the Worcester Board of Trade in 1903. In 1905, Goddard entertained President Taft, then Secretary of War, at "Elmarion." Upon the death of Eleanor Goddard Daniels in 1981 (the last surviving child of Harry Goddard and owner of the house), her will bequeathed 190 Salisbury Street to the American Antiquarian Society across the street. It now serves as an educational center and residence for visiting scholars to the Antiquarian Society.

Aldus Higgins House (1921)
1 John Wing Road
Grosvenor Atterbury (New York)

Aldus Higgins House
102-M

The Aldus Higgins House at 1 John Wing Road, opposite Institute Park, was begun in 1921 and completed two years later. It is the most interesting and elaborate of Worcester's early 20th century period houses. Although plans were prepared by Grosvenor Atterbury of New York, Aldus Higgins is believed to have spent a number of years making sketches and gathering materials from Europe for the house prior to hiring Atterbury. Unlike two other major "period" residences in Worcester (Knollwood at 425 Salisbury Street, and the Paul Morgan House at 21 Cedar Street), the Higgins House is known to contain some antique European building materials.

The entry facade consists of two wings (set perpendicularly to each other) containing a semi-octagonal entry tower (with crenellations) at the wings' junction. Throughout, the building is constructed of various materials following the general pattern of stone (1st storey), half-timbering with brick panels (2nd storey), and half-timbering with stucco panels (gables).

The building's garden facade also is made up of two wings, joined at right angles by a two storey gabled pavilion which contains a two storey window with ornate tracery.

Other features of the exterior include ornate chimney pots and elaborate foliate decoration in the stucco of the half-timbering. Of much smaller scale, the garage bears the same design elements as the house. Connecting the two structures and surrounding the house are original garden walls, gates and terraces.

Aldus Higgins (born 1872) was a son of Milton Prince Higgins, superintendent of the Washburn Shops at Worcester Polytechnic Institute and a founder of several major local industries, including Norton Company, Plunger Elevator Company, Riley Stoker Corporation and Worcester Pressed Steel Company. The younger Higgins attended Worcester Polytechnic Institute, from which he graduated in 1893. Aldus Higgins studied law in Washington, D.C., and served as an assistant examiner in the United States Patent Office. In 1896, Mr. Higgins was admitted to the bar, and opened a law office in Worcester in 1897. He gave up his private practice to serve as general counsel for the Norton Company during a period of growth and reorganization of the firm. He became the company's president and chairman, also serving as treasurer of Riley Stoker Corporation.

The house is now owned and well cared for by Worcester Polytechnic Institute.

Bliss Building (1888)
26 Old Lincoln Street
Barker & Nourse

Bliss Building
103-B

Designed by the architectural firm of Barker & Nourse, and built in 1888, the Bliss Building is a four storey brick block of rectangular plan. The facade is symmetrical rising from a foundation of rock-faced sandstone to a brick and sandstone parapet which bears a name plaque. The center entry is framed by square columns with channeling and rosettes. Window trim varies by storey, although all is made of rock-faced sandstone. Beginning at the top of the first storey, two brick piers divide the wall into three sections. These piers rise to terra cotta ventilators above the parapet. Other decorations of the facade include terra cotta tiles and a sandstone date plaque. Sidewalls of the Bliss Building are undecorated and were originally concealed by neighboring structures.

Located immediately north of Lincoln Square, the Bliss Building was once part of an early district of brick apartment houses built largely in the 1880s. During the twentieth century, highway construction, urban renewal and the area's residential decline resulted in the demolition of virtually all other buildings of this type around Lincoln Square. The Bliss Building was constructed for William Bliss, son of Harrison Bliss, both of whom were real estate developers in the Lincoln Square and downtown sections of Worcester. It is currently in original condition.

Charles Miles House (1850)
131 Lincoln Street

Together with the John Hammond House (264 Highland Street), which it resembles, the Charles Miles House is one of Worcester's best examples of Italianate residential architecture. The house is made up of a two storey front section with a hip roof and rock-faced granite foundation, and a rear ell centered in the east wall of the front section. Among the fine details this house exhibits are: corner quoins, a modillioned cornice, "widow's walk" framed by a balustrade, bay windows, and window caps set on consoles. An especially fine detail is the original porch framed by arched openings.

Around 1846 a house on the opposite corner of Forestdale Road was purchased by Willard Miles. Between 1847 and 1849 Charles Miles, a clerk in the Worcester County Treasurer's Office, was listed in local directories as a boarder at Willard Miles's house. The change in Charles Miles's listing to a separate house on Lincoln Street (1850), and the appearance of a house on this site on the 1851 map of Worcester, suggest the building's construction date. The architect, if any, is unknown.

Charles Miles House
90-B-2

Fred Harris Daniels House (1885)
148 Lincoln Street

Built in 1885, the Daniels House is an excellent example of Queen Anne style architecture. Asymmetrical in plan and massing, the house rises from a brick first storey which is trimmed with rock-faced sandstone and terra cotta tiles. The second floor and attic are of frame construction covered with clapboards and decorative shingling. Characteristic of much Queen Anne design, the house has first and second storey porches in its south wall and an entry porch bearing a sunburst decoration in its gable on the facade. An additional sunburst decorates the facade's first storey, arched window. At present, the Daniels House is in original condition.

The house was first occupied by Fred Harris Daniels (1853–1913). Daniels, the son of a contractor, was brought to Worcester at the age of one year. In 1873 he

Fred Harris Daniels House
90-D

graduated from Worcester Polytechnic Institute and immediately entered the employ of Washburn and Moen Company. Around 1875–1876 Daniels was sent to Philadelphia to study steel-making, in an effort to improve the quality of steel produced at the Washburn and Moen factory. In 1877 Daniels traveled throughout Europe, studying the production of steel. Having occupied various positions at Washburn and Moen, Daniels was made general superintendent of the company in 1888.

Draper Ruggles House (1848)
21 Catharine Street

Draper Ruggles House
103-G

The Draper Ruggles House is an important local example of Greek Revival architecture. Basically square in plan, with a rear ell, the house rises two storeys from a rock-faced granite foundation to a low hip roof. The symmetrical facade has a two storey portico supported by reeded columns. The center bay of the portico has a projecting entry pavilion which is framed by pilasters with a balcony at the second storey. The portico's columns and the pilasters support a wide entablature and cornice. Alterations consist of a two storey porch on the west elevation (ca. 1910–1930), exterior wooden stairs on the east elevation (ca. 1960), and a Victorian entry hood and double doors (ca. 1880). With the exception of the Victorian entry, no alterations have been made to the original fabric of the building.

The Ruggles House is a rare survivor of a type of Greek Revival house (hip roof, square plan, two storey portico) which was popularized by Elias Carter, an early local architect. Although many houses of this type were built in the 1830s and 1840s, only the Dowley-Taylor House, the Levi Lincoln House (moved to Sturbridge Village), and the Ruggles House remain substantially intact. Although no architect is known for the Ruggles House, the building's overall appearance and its unusual reeded columns suggest Carter, who is known to have returned to this area in the late 1840s to supervise construction of the Lyman School for Boys in Westborough. Shown on the 1851 map of Worcester, the Ruggles House is likely to have been built shortly after 1848 when much of the surrounding area (northward to Grant Square) was opened for development.

Draper Ruggles was a member of the manufacturing firm of Ruggles, Nourse & Mason. Located in rented space in the Court Mills (demolished), the firm purchased a patent for "the most improved form of cast-iron plow" from Jethro Wood in 1838 and added it to their line of agricultural implements. In 1856 Ruggles withdrew from the firm, and later the company was purchased by Oliver Ames of Boston. During the second quarter of the nineteenth century Ruggles, Nourse & Mason was one of the largest manufacturers of agricultural implements in Worcester, at a time when the city led the nation in this line of manufacturing.

In the 1860s the house passed into the possession of Jesse Moore (occupation unknown). Moore lived in the Ruggles House until around 1892, when he moved into 25 Catharine Street. Prior to the construction of 25 Catharine Street, the Ruggles House was located further east, toward Windsor Street. Around 1889–1890 it was moved westward on its original lot, to its present location.

Jesse Moore House (1890)
25 Catharine Street

The Jesse Moore House, under construction in 1890 and occupied in 1891, is a superb local example of Queen Anne style architecture, one which also contains elements of Shingle Style design. The house is of asymmetrical plan rising from a basement and first storey of rock-faced granite, laid in a broken course, to a second storey of frame construction covered with shingles. The building's complex roof is slate-covered. The facade has a large, three storey octagonal tower at its southwest corner and a small octagonal tower at its southeast corner. Extending along the facade is an open porch, above which is a recessed porch at the second storey, between the towers. Both east and west elevations carry the same decorative elements as the facade, including terra cotta tiles varied (decorative) sash, dormers and porches. The Moore House is unaltered except for the addition of a fire escape on its west elevation.

Jesse Moore first moved to 25 Catharine Street about 1861 when the Draper Ruggles House stood on this lot. Around 1889, Moore had the Ruggles House moved westward on the lot to its present site and construction was begun on Moore's new house. The Moore House remained in the Moore family until 1925

Jesse Moore House
103-H

when it was purchased by the Louis Pasteur Hospital Association and converted to a hospital for the city's large French-Canadian population. It is now a nursing home.

"Soho Cottage" (1860)
21 Windsor Street

"Soho Cottage"
90-G-7

"Soho Cottage" at 21 Windsor Street is the best example of early Gothic Revival extant in Worcester. Often called Carpenter Gothic, ornamentation of the building is elaborate. Gables with ornate bargeboards, ogee arched windows, entry porches with pierced brackets, plus board and batten siding are classic elements of this architectural style.

The cottage was purchased by William Allen in 1860 shortly after it was built for $1,250 by real estate developer Samuel Davis. Allen was a native of Soho, England who came to Worcester in 1849 as a young machinist. During the '60s, Allen was a foreman at the Court Mills for Nourse, Mason & Company, later the Ames Plow Company. In 1872 he became partner in the Stewart & Allen Boiler Works which was dissolved in 1875, the same year in which Allen bought the Worcester Boiler Works. Renamed William Allen & Sons in 1898 when it became one of the largest manufacturers of steam boilers in New England, Allen was still living in "Soho Cottage" when he died in 1906.

"Forest Hill Cottage" (1860)
22 Windsor Street

Built as a mirror image of its neighbor, "Soho Cottage," "Forest Hill Cottage" is among Worcester's best examples of Carpenter Gothic architecture. The house is symmetrical in plan and massing, rising one and one half storeys from a brick foundation to steeply pitched roofs. Portions of the building contain an attic above the upper storey. Major features of the house are its deep eaves (bargeboards removed), board and batten siding, bay window, and facade gable which contains an ogee-arch window. Around 1880–1890, the present front porch (semi-octagonal in plan) was added.

Purchased by Luther Ross from Samuel Davis, a real estate developer, for $1,250 in 1860, 22 Windsor Street was first named "Forest Hill Cottage" in the city directory of 1861. The hillside site, fanciful architecture and name are characteristic of the surrounding area's mid-nineteenth century development which was heavily influenced by Romantic ideas regarding landscape and architecture. Luther Ross was a pattern maker who worked at the Court Mills, probably in the employ of Nourse, Mason & Company. Ross occupied "Forest Hill Cottage" until 1886 when it was sold to H. D. Gough, whose heirs retained ownership of the property into the twentieth century.

"Forest Hill Cottage"
90-G-8

Prentiss-Hanson House (1877)
3 Channing Way

Located on a hilltop approximately 40' above Kendall Street, the Prentiss-Hanson House is an important local example of Victorian Gothic architecture. The house is of brick construction, two and one half storeys high with gabled slate roofs. The main facade is symmetrical with a three and one half storey tower at its center and an open porch extending its length. The tower rises to a high hip roof with jerkinhead dormers on each side. The building's north elevation contains an original open porch and entry, which seems likely to have been the major entry. The steep slope of the facade makes the facade main entry inaccessible.

It was built for Addison Prentiss (1815–1895), a local publisher who came to Worcester in 1851–1852. Until 1866 Prentiss worked as a designer, lithographer and engraver, producing (among other views) an important 1851 view of Worcester from Court Hill. After 1866, he became a book dealer and later a publisher. Prentiss occupied 3 Channing Way until 1887 when he sold it to Charles F. Hanson. Hanson, reputed to be Worcester's first Swedish immigrant, came here in 1868 at the age of nineteen years. Having worked as a piano tuner and repairman for S. R. Leland and Co., Hanson in 1870 opened his own business, selling pianos, musical instruments and "musical merchandise." Active in local Swedish organizations, Hanson became one of the wealthiest and most influential members of Worcester's large Swedish community.

Prentiss-Hanson House
103-J

D. Wheeler Swift House
103-L

D. Wheeler Swift House (1879)
22 Oak Avenue

Built in 1879–1880, the Swift House is an unaltered example of its period, bearing elements of Victorian Gothic and Stick Style design. Two and one half storeys high, the facade is dominated by a steep gable with decorative bargeboards and apron, elements which are repeated on a smaller gable on the north elevation. An unusual detail of the design, is the entry which is set at a 45 degree angle to the building's north and west elevations. On either side of the entry is an original porch with open braces and geometric railing. Other original details include window caps, granite stoop, and a low retaining wall of rock-faced granite along the property's Oak Avenue and Kendall Street fronts.

D. Wheeler Swift (1840–1910) was a native of West Falmouth, Massachusetts, who came to Worcester in 1864 to operate envelope-making machinery at the newly formed Bay State Envelope Company. Together with his brother, Henry D. Swift, he invented various envelope-making machines upon which the success of the Whitcomb Envelope Company and, later, the Logan, Swift and Brigham Envelope Company was based.

Bentley-Jackson Cottage (ca. 1850)
9 Earle Street

The Bentley-Jackson Cottage is one of Worcester's best remaining examples of Carpenter Gothic architecture. The cottage is one and one half storeys high with an attic beneath a steeply pitched roof. It has a side-hall floor plan and is flanked by open porches with chamfered posts, brackets and railings of turned balusters. Except for the front door (replaced 1880s) all the Gothic features of the house are intact, including bargeboards, label mouldings and gabled dormers which are cantilevered out through the eaves. Apparent alterations of the 1880s brought about the addition of a second storey to the facade's bay window as well as the addition of decorative shingling (gable only) and the present front door and entry hood. While these additions are Queen Anne in style, they do not interfere with the

Bentley-Jackson Cottage
103-M-1

building's original features which serve more as evolutionary changes than as intrusions.

Characteristic of much of the cottage building which occurred at the base of Chandler Hill in the 1840s and 1850s, the Bentley-Jackson Cottage is the area's best preserved survivor from its initial period of suburbanization. The lot on which the house stands was purchased by John Bartlett in June of 1849, at which time it contained no buildings. Late in May of 1850, Bartlett sold the lot and buildings to George Bentley and Daniel H. Jackson, both clerks at the office of the Superintendent of the Nashua Railroad. Bentley and Jackson were first listed at 9 Earle Street in the directory of 1851.

Joel Flagg House (ca. 1849)
15 Elizabeth Street

The Joel Flagg House is an excellent local example of Greek Revival style architecture, consisting of a two storey frame structure with a side hall floor plan. The facade is framed by corner pilasters supporting an entablature and cornice which are carried across the gable to give the appearance of a pediment. Extending around the west and south sides is an open Doric porch behind which the first storey has oversized 6/6 windows. Except for a small shed dormer on its south side, the Flagg house is substantially unaltered.

Once a common building type, particularly during the 1840s and 1850s when hillsides around the central business district became the city's first suburbs, Greek Revival style houses such as 15 Elizabeth Street have become increasingly rare. Together with the nearby Leonard Sturtevant House, the Flagg House is among the last unaltered buildings of the 1840s and 1850s left on Chandler Hill. The lot on which the house stands was sold to Joel Flagg by David Messinger, a land speculator, in May of 1848. By 1849, the house was occupied by Flagg who lived here until his death (ca. 1854), after which it was sold to George Gale, a paper manufacturer, in 1859. Gale occupied the house from 1860 until the turn of the century.

Joel Flagg House
103-M-2

Borden-Pond House
117-E

Borden-Pond House (1856–58)
40 Laurel Street

Built between 1856 and 1859 and (perhaps) completed in the 1860s, the Borden-Pond House is an early, important example of Second Empire style architecture, one which retains architectural significance despite alteration. The front (original) section of the house is contructed of granite rubble with dressed quoins and window trim. The house rises from a high basement two storeys to a modillioned cornice, above which the original concavely curved mansard has been squared out to create a full third storey. The facade is approached by two symmetrical, curved granite stairways which retain fine cast-iron railings. At the facade's center is a two storey pavilion in front of which is an entry porch with arched openings (now glazed). Flanking this pavilion are two porches, enclosed by modern siding which covers the original trim. Located on the west slope of Chandler Hill, the Borden-Pond House is among Worcester's few remaining stone "villas" of the 1850s and 1860s, although a large number of them (both in Italianate and Second Empire styles) once stood on the hills which surround the city's center.

The Borden-Pond House was built for (and perhaps by) John Borden, who is listed variously in city directories as a mason, stucco worker, and as a mastic and stucco worker. Borden only occupied the house until 1860–1861. Local tradition suggests that in building 40 Laurel Street, Borden intended to outdo the opulence of the nearby Merrifield House (now demolished). Further, it is believed that Borden could not afford to complete the house and that it was sold, unfinished, to Lucius Pond in 1861.

According to local directories, Lucius Pond (1826–1888) lived in the Borden-Pond House from 1868–1875 when he was sent to prison. Pond was a native of Hubbardston, Massachusetts who came to Worcester in 1846. Having learned the machinist's trade of Samuel Flagg, Pond entered into partnership with Flagg between 1847 and 1849. In 1859 Pond became sole owner of the business, which was moved in 1859 to the Merrifield Building where Pond manufactured engine-lathes, planing machines and other heavy equipment. During this period Pond became an important local machine manufacturer, owning some of the most advanced equipment of the time. At the outbreak of the Civil War, Pond invented the "Ellsworth Gun" (a canon capable of shooting an 18 oz. ball three miles) which he manufactured for the Union Army.

In 1858–1859 Pond was a member of the common council, in 1862 an alderman and in 1866–1868 a state senator. He was an early member of the Laurel Street Methodist Church and became known for his financial generosity. Pond was a director of the Central National Bank from 1866 to 1875 when rumors of the insolvency of his business led to his departure from Worcester on a business trip. Travelling to New York by steamship, Pond left the ship in disguise, leaving belongings in his cabin in such a way as to suggest suicide by having jumped overboard. After a lengthy search Pond was arrested in San Francisco as he was about to board a boat to Australia. Having been brought back to Worcester, Pond was convicted of forging dates on bank notes and sentenced to a fifteen-year prison term. Despite the widespread losses caused by Pond's fraud, petitions on behalf of his parole were circulated until he was released from prison in 1882.

Upon his return from prison, a number of Pond's friends purchased the Powell Machine Company, re-naming it the L. W. Pond Machine Company, and offered Pond the job of superintendent. Although he never recovered his earlier business prominence, Lucius Pond regained much of his earlier popularity and at his death in 1888 was the subject of laudatory obituaries.

Leonard Sturtevant House (ca. 1849)
84 Mulberry Street

First occupied in 1849, the Sturtevant House is a unique local example of Greek Revival architecture. The house is a two storey frame structure with a "T"-shaped floor plan, each wing of which is trimmed with corner pilasters and a pedimented gable. The side-hall facade has an original entry and windows set in earred frames with splayed sides. Extending along the facade and side walls of the house is an open Doric porch set in a granite base. Pedimented gables contain an arched window with label moulding and octagonal lights. Set over the crossing of the building's floor plan is a square cupola. Although covered by asbestos siding, the Sturtevant House remains intact.

Leonard Sturtevant, a tailor who owned the house during the last half of the

Leonard Sturtevant House
117-F

nineteenth century, is characteristic of the middle class businessmen and small-scale manufacturers who settled in the vicinity of Belmont Hill during the 1840s and 1850s. Lured by the picturesque potential of hillside sites, the first occupants of Belmont Hill built cottages and moderate-sized houses in the then popular Gothic and Greek Revival styles. The area's popularity was relatively short-lived, and by the 1870s and 1880s it was being more densely built up with working-class housing. One possible reason for the area's abandonment by the middle-class residents may have been its position immediately east of a major industrial district, the fumes from which would have been carried over Belmont Hill by prevailing winds. In addition, the area was immediately northeast of a large district of immigrants (Pine Meadow) which was seen as a major social problem as early as the 1850s. Subsequent development has obscured much of the early history of Belmont Hill, leaving the Sturtevant House an important reminder of the area's past.

Richard Barker House (1855)
312 Plantation Street

The Richard Barker House is a rare example of the so-called Octagonal Mode popular in the 1850s and early 1860s. There are only two left in Worcester. The other is the Elias Crawford House at 3 Norwood Street. Built about 1865–1866, the first known occupant was Richard Barker, a carpenter, who first lived in the house in 1866. Constructed of stone chips faced with stucco incised to resemble masonry, the building's eight outside walls have pilaster-like raised sections at the heads of which are paired brackets. Prior to the 1920s, this house had an octagonal cupola.

The Octagonal Mode became faddish as a result of books by Orson Squire Fowler. One in particular—"A House for All, or the Gravel Wall and Octagon Mode of Building, New, Cheap, Convenient, Superior and Adapted to Rich and Poor"—went through eight printings between 1848–1857. Although Fowler recommended stone and mortar ("the gravel wall"), most octagonal houses were built of wood. Hence, examples of gravel wall construction, such as this Barker house, are very rare in Worcester or anywhere else.

Richard Barker House
119-A

"Larchmont" (1858)
36 Butler Street
Elbridge Boyden

"Larchmont"
191-A

Located on a hillside in what was countryside in the 1850s, "Larchmont" is a rare survivor of the many Italianate and Second Empire style villas which dotted the hillsides around Worcester in the 1850s and 1860s. Built as the country home of Ransom C. Taylor, the house is a two storey frame structure, set on a granite foundation. The facade is symmetrical above a slightly projecting central pavilion with a low gable. At the first storey of the pavilion is an original bracketed entry porch (glazing added) and arched entry; at the second storey is a Palladian window with a moulded cap set on consoles; and at the third storey an oculus. Symmetrical porches with brackets and original balustrades are at either end of the facade. Alterations to the building include the removal of its original octagonal cupola, the addition of a porte cochère, and the installation of aluminum siding (no details were removed for the siding). Despite these alterations, "Larchmont" remains among the city's finest examples of Italianate architecture.

It seems likely that "Larchmont" was designed by Elbridge Boyden, architect of Mechanics Hall, although the reference is somewhat confused. The obituary of Elbridge Boyden notes that Boyden designed the "present residence of R. C. Taylor" (1898). As Taylor's home in 1898 was a house known to have been designed by Elias Carter and built in 1842 for Levi Dowley, it is likely that the obituary reference was meant to indicate "Larchmont" which was then a residence of R. F. Taylor, son of Ransom C. Taylor. Supportive of a Boyden attribution are details of "Larchmont" which resemble other known Boyden designs of the 1850s.

Ransom Taylor was born in Winchester, New Hampshire in 1829, and as a child moved to Northbridge, Massachusetts where his father was in the meat business. Around 1851, Taylor moved to Worcester where he lived until his death in 1898. Taylor's first listing in local directories (1853) gives his occupation as "Tripe Manufacturer" in the Quinsigamond area of the city (where "Larchmont" is located). It seems clear that he also became involved in real estate speculation and development soon after his arrival. According to his obituary, Taylor made a practice of purchasing as much land as he could, and, as the city's population boomed, saw the value of his investments more than double itself. As the city's largest property holder, Taylor built the city's first seven storey block along with many other buildings in the downtown area. From 1858 until 1883 Taylor lived at "Larchmont." After 1883 he occupied the Dowley-Taylor Mansion at 770 Main Street.

Salisbury House (1836–38)
61 Harvard Street

Salisbury House
102-N

The Salisbury House is situated on high ground in downtown Worcester on a block bounded by Highland Street, Harvard Street, Institute Road, and Lancaster Street. It was moved a few feet northwest from its original site in 1931 to prevent demolition when Harvard Street was widened.

Built for Stephen Salisbury II in 1836–38 by Elias Carter, a master builder, this house has been called the best of Carter's Worcester buildings. The two and one half storey wood frame, hip roof building is Greek Revival in style with details used freely rather than academically in effecting a design of classic elegance and simplicity. Piers support a full entablature, though one without frieze or architrave divisions. Little exterior ornament was used, being confined to a smooth ashlar treatment of the wood sheathing, wreathed oculus windows in the frieze, and the use of label molding over the second floor windows. The west facade and east elevation are crossed by one storey fluted Doric columned porches. A three bay conservatory of the same height and with Doric pilasters is attached to the south elevation. The north elevation except for smooth imitation ashlar quoins, is flush boarded. The ell, apparently original, is an unarticulated addition which has been altered through the years.

The significance of the Salisbury House derives both from architectural significance and associations with the original owner. Built to emphasize Stephen II's rising position in the community as a wealthy man of New England, the house became a landmark in the city, and was frequently reproduced in panoramic views of the town and in local histories.

An unusual example of Greek Revival style, it adheres to the principles of classical design and unity. Of particular note is the circular composition of the spiral staircase, and rotunda surrounding it, in the central hall. This house is considered to be one of the finest of the many grand houses erected during this time of prosperity in Worcester, and was a fitting residence for the Salisbury family.

Stephen III continued to live in the house after his father's death in 1884. He carried on his father's tradition in the community and was active in the founding of the Worcester Art Museum in 1896. He gave generously to many other cultural institutions in Worcester, and when he died in 1905 he left the Salisbury House to the Trustees of the Worcester Art Museum. In 1907 the building became part of the Art Museum School. The Museum School remained in the building until 1939, and in 1941 the Worcester Chapter of the American Red Cross bought the building. The house was refitted as the headquarters of the Chapter with complete sympathy for the architectural merit of the building. It is a good example of sensitive re-use of an architecturally significant structure.

Whitcomb House (1879)
51 Harvard Street
Stephen C. Earle

Perhaps the finest example of a high Victorian mansion in Worcester is the Whitcomb House at the corner of Highland and Harvard Streets. Built in 1879–80 for George Henry Whitcomb, businessman-philanthropist, it was lived in by his family until 1918 when given to the Memorial Homes for the Blind.

One of the few remaining residential houses designed by Worcester architect Stephen C. Earle, the Whitcomb House is both architecturally and historically significant. Asymmetrical and polychromatic in style similar to Queen Anne (with Gothic overtones), it is a three storey granite structure with picturesque roofline composed of many dormers. The house is adjoined by several porches, verandas and a conservatory, and is surrounded on the north and east by a low stone fence.

Dominated by a three storey central gabled wing, the facade is made up of vertical planes. The top of the wing, within the gable, is decorated with diaper work framed (at the roof's edge) by a coping of light colored stone. This central wing contains the main entrance formed by a round arch supported by two carved Gothic style granite columns. A second storey balcony of ornamented cast iron rests on heavy carved stone brackets above the door which creates an entrance shelter. The corners of the facade are rounded with a three storey turret and conical slate roof on the right and a gently sloped, cut-away corner on the left.

The interior retains most of the original floor plan plus details of the very elegant wood paneling and decorations. The formal first floor rooms are finished in cherry, oak, butternut and mahogany. Tile, terra cotta and marble frame the fireplaces. The second floor rooms are finished in cherry, ash and maple. Behind stands a handsome, single storey, stone stable and carriage house well matched in style to the main house.

Mr. Whitcomb was born in Templeton (1842) and educated at Andover and Amherst. He founded the Bay State Envelope Company in Worcester as a one-man operation which blossomed into a large and profitable enterprise manufacturing one third of all staple envelopes used in the United States. He sold the business to the U.S. Envelope Company in 1898.

Whitcomb House
102-S

Salem Copeland House
116-B

Salem Copeland House
31 Harvard Street

The Copeland House is one of the most ornate, temple front Greek Revival houses left in Worcester. The other is the Arad Alexander House at 53 Waverly Street. Nowhere in the city can the quality and abundance of their ornamentation be equalled. It is very possible that Mr. Copeland, a builder, designed and built this house himself about 1847. By 1870, he had moved to Wachusett Street having sold his Harvard Street house to Horace Sheldon, the owner of a dry goods store in Mechanics Hall. The house was sold again in the 1880s to E. A. Brown who had previously owned the house at 25 Harvard Street.

The exterior of the Copeland House is clapboard; the stable brick. A pedimented facade displays composite (a modification of Corinthian) capitals with anthemia (stylized honeysuckle flower design) and scrollwork decoration around gable windows.

Goulding House (1840s)
4 Dix Street

The Goulding House at 4 Dix Street is a two storey Greek Revival frame house set on a foundation of rock-faced granite. Made up of three bays with a side hall entry, the facade is framed by corner pilasters supporting an entablature and cornice which extend across the gable to create a pediment. At the first storey is an open porch supported by four fluted Ionic columns. The major entry is set in a pilastered frame with side lights and an original four-panel door.

The Goulding House was built originally around 1848 at 26 Harvard Street for Henry Goulding, the machinery manufacturer and a founder of the Worcester Mechanics Association. Goulding's woolen machinery business was purchased by Willard Williams and Company, perhaps at a large profit, which led Henry Goulding to move this house in 1849 to its present site at 4 Dix Street and to build the large Italianate mansion at 26 Harvard Street. When located at 4 Dix Street, the house was sold to Samuel Bemis (1850) and later to David Whiting Eames, Bemis's son-in-law.

Goulding House
116-E

Henry Goulding Mansion (1850)
26 Harvard Street

M. G. Wheelock (Boston)

Henry Goulding Mansion
116-C

Believed to have been designed by M. G. Wheelock of Boston (earlier of Barre, Mass.) and constructed by Captain Edwin Lamb of Worcester in 1850–1851, the Henry Goulding Mansion was one of the most opulent, Italianate style houses built in Worcester during the mid-nineteenth century. It is two storeys high, of frame construction, with a low hip roof. The symmetrical facade contains a fine original entry porch with arched openings, modillioned cornice and parapet. First storey windows are set in moulded architraves with consoles supporting pedimented caps; second storey windows are set in nearly identical surrounds without pediments. Extending around the building is a panelled and bracketed cornice. Prior to the conversion of the house to a home for the aged, its exterior was covered with wood (probably clapboards) and had corner quoins. Originally the house had a cupola which was removed after 1927. Attached to the south wall is a two storey brick addition with a facade of equal-sized bays. Of eclectic style, this addition is covered with stucco and has arched windows, decorative brickwork, cornice brackets and a slate-covered hip roof. At the south end of the 1926 addition is a new wing of modern design completed in 1978. The Goulding Mansion was built for Henry Goulding on the site of his earlier Greek Revival style house which was moved to 4 Dix Street.

Henry Goulding was an early local manufacturer of woolen machinery. In 1831, he was one of several partners who bought the woolen machine business of Washburn & Goddard. Under a series of different partnerships and occasionally under his sole ownership, Goulding developed the business into one of Worcester's largest machine manufacturers. Goulding was also a Worcester selectman, a founder and president of Mechanics National Bank, and a founder of the Worcester Mechanics Association. In 1851 Goulding sold the firm to Willard Williams & Company and "retired with a fortune" to this house on Harvard Street where he lived until his death in 1866.

Otis Putnam House
116-D

Otis Putnam House (1887)
25 Harvard Street
Fuller & Delano

Built in 1887, from designs by Fuller & Delano, the Otis Putnam House is a good local example of Queen Anne style architecture, one which retains excellent stained glass. Two and one half storeys high, the Putnam House is built of pressed brick, set on a foundation of rock-faced granite laid in a broken course. The asymmetrical facade has first and second storey porches with original trim, above which is a high gable with a central oriel and shingles set in an undulating pattern. Side elevations of the house bear the same decorative details. Surrounding the property is an original granite retaining wall. The Putnam House was built on a lot which Otis Putnam bought from the heirs of T. E. Hall. Shortly after the purchase, Putnam had an existing Greek Revival style house moved to the rear of the lot (now 1 Dix Street), and construction began on the present house which remains unaltered.

Putnam, a native of Leicester, was born in 1831 and began work in 1847 as a clerk in the store of John B. Wyman in Worcester. Putnam remained with the business through several changes of ownership during which the firm name was changed to H. H. Chamberlain and Company (1850), Chamberlain, Barnard & Company (1857), and after the admission of Putnam to the firm, Barnard, Sumner & Putnam. In the last quarter of the nineteenth century the business grew rapidly, becoming one of the city's largest department stores.

Jerome Marble House (1867)
23 Harvard Street
Elbridge Boyden

Built in 1867 and designed by Elbridge Boyden, the Jerome Marble House is an excellent local example of Second Empire style architecture, and one of the few buildings of its style for which an architect has been identified. Built of pressed brick, the house is two and one half storeys high with a slate-covered mansard roof. The facade is symmetrical with a center entrance flanked by three-sided bay windows. The roof bears a variety of gabled and arched dormers. With the exception of a modern front door, the Marble House is unaltered and in excellent condition. The property also retains an original granite stoop, rock-faced granite retaining wall, and granite gate posts.

Jerome Marble (1824–1906) was a native of Charlton, Massachusetts who came to Worcester in 1853, becoming a business partner of C. A. Harrington. In 1863 the company became Jerome Marble & Company, "druggists and dealers in paints and oils, chemicals, etc." He was a director of the Quinsigamond Bank, and much involved in efforts to establish "the first excursion car business in the country" under the name of the Worcester Excursion Car Company—an effort which eventually failed when the company was denied the use of railroad beds.

Jerome Marble House
116-G

Tilley Raymond House (1848)
12 George Street

The Tilley Raymond House was built in 1847. It is a fine example of the once popular side-hall type of Greek Revival style house. The building is two and one half storeys high, built on a foundation of rock-faced granite. The facade is three bays wide with corner pilasters and a pedimented gable. Across the first storey of the facade is a Doric porch, behind which the landing is covered with matched boarding. The entry contains paired replacement doors (ca. 1875). Sash throughout is original 6/6 except for the facade first storey where original over-sized windows contain 6/9 sash.

A native of Royalston, Massachusetts, Tilley Raymond (b. 1812) came to Worcester in 1834 and worked locally as a carpenter. By the 1840s Raymond had entered into partnership with Horatio Tower as Tower & Raymond, Worcester's most active builders of the 1840s and 1850s. Among the most well-known buildings constructed by the firm are the Old Central Church (demolished) and Mechanics Hall. In addition to working in Worcester, Raymond is known to have been in California in 1851, perhaps to take advantage of the building boom which followed the gold rush. After Raymond's death, 12 George Street was occupied by his son Edward, who had served in the Civil War and later became Chief of Police in

Tilley Raymond House
116-I

Worcester and Clerk of Worcester's Central District Court. The younger Raymond studied law with Senator George Hoar of Worcester and was admitted to the bar in 1880. In 1898 the house was sold to Henry E. Whitcomb who converted it to apartments.

Governor Levi Lincoln House (1834)
4 Avalon Place
Elias Carter

Governor Levi Lincoln House
116-L-6

Built in 1834, the Governor Levi Lincoln House is Worcester's earliest example of the side-hall Greek Revival style of house, a style which dominated local building in the 1840s and 1850s. Exhibiting elements of late Federalist architecture, the Lincoln House rests on a foundation of hammered granite. It has narrow corner boards and moulded window trim. Characteristic of the Greek Revival style, the facade gable is made to appear as a pediment by the extension of a cornice across its length. Further Greek Revival elements include the pedimented entry porch with Doric columns and the front doorway with sidelights, a rectangular top light, and an original four-panel door.

Levi Lincoln, Jr. (1782–1868) was born in Worcester the son of Levi Lincoln, a prominent lawyer. Levi, Jr. graduated from Harvard in 1802 and began the study of law under his father, then the Attorney General of the United States. In 1805 he was admitted to the bar, opened an office in Worcester, and by 1812 had been elected to the State Senate. In 1814 he was elected to the Massachusetts House of Representatives, serving for seven years. Lincoln was elected Governor of Massachusetts in 1825, serving nine consecutive years in that office. After stepping down from the governorship (1834), Lincoln was appointed to fill out a vacancy in the U.S. House of Representatives, a position to which he was elected in 1835.

Lincoln decided to retire to Worcester in 1834 at which time he commissioned Elias Carter, a local architect, to design a mansion for his Elm Street estate. Number 4 Avalon Place was constructed in the "east garden" to provide Lincoln with a dwelling during the construction of the main house which was not completed until late in 1838. Lincoln served as the city's first mayor in 1848.

Upon moving into the larger house, Lincoln sold this building to John

Richardson of Newton whose son, George, a Worcester lawyer, occupied the house for forty years. In 1878, the house and its lot were sold to Jonas Clark who built a house on the site, selling the Lincoln House to Col. William A. Williams who moved it to its present site and converted it into apartments.

The Lincoln Mansion is now part of Old Sturbridge Village.

Marcus Hobbs House (1849)
16 William Street

The Marcus Hobbs House dates from 1849. It is a two storey structure with a side-hall floor plan. The gabled facade has a Doric porch (first storey), over-sized windows, corner pilasters, and an arched window in the gable. Apparent alterations to the house (ca. 1870) include the extension of the original porch around the west side, paired brackets at the cornice, cornice dentils and, perhaps, the gable window. Restored in 1979, the house remains unaltered from ca. 1870.

The Hobbs House is located in an area which was developed primarily by carpenters from the late 1840s until the mid–1870s. Located at the eastern end of Bowdoin, William and John Streets, this area has been fragmented by modern highway and parking lot construction, leaving few examples of the earlier use. The Hobbs House was built in 1849 by Marcus Hobbs, a carpenter, who occupied the property from 1849 until 1861 when he sold the house to Silas Batchelor, also a carpenter. In the 1860s the property changed hands several times until it was sold to Edward Hamilton, a music teacher, assistant treasurer of the Worcester County Institution for Savings, and founder of the Mozart Society in Worcester. Following Hamilton's death in 1870, the property was bought by John F. Adams, who sold off the rear portion of the lot to Henry Palmer (a builder) in 1873. Adams seems likely to have remodeled the house slightly, adding its present Victorian features. Adams and his heirs retained ownership of the house well into the twentieth century. The Hobbs House is an excellent example of mid-nineteenth century, middle-class housing.

Marcus Hobbs House
116-L-36

George Cobb House
116-L-4

George Cobb House (1875)
24 William Street

First occupied in 1875, the George Cobb House is an ornate and unaltered example of Victorian Gothic architecture. The structure is two and one half storeys high, rising from a foundation of rock-faced granite to a slate-covered hip roof with decorative gabled pavilion at its center. Set in the first storey of the pavilion is the main entry framed by an ogee arch and clustered columns. Flanking the entry are three-sided bay windows which are connected by a three-sided open porch with a railing of quatrefoil panels. Above the entry is a tripartite arched window, capped by a stylized ogee arch. The pavilion's gable is trimmed by an apron pierced with trefoils, and by bargeboards which terminate in quatrefoils. Dormers are trimmed with similar decoration. First storey windows on the side elevations have gabled caps with incised decoration. The second storey windows have moulded caps on consoles and stylized volutes at their bases.

The Cobb House's first occupant was George Cobb, a fish and oyster merchant, who owned the house into the early twentieth century. No architect has been identified.

John Hastings Cottage (1880)
31 William Street

Built about 1880, this fanciful and ornate house is a rare example of a period which saw the design and construction (especially in the northeast U.S.) of many rural and suburban cottages of the Hudson River School. The term "cottage" describes the smaller, less pretentious cousin of the villas and town houses of the same school.

The Hastings house rests on an original foundation of "cast-stone" (concrete) rising one and one half storeys to a complex hip roof covered with fish-scale slates. Above the roof is an octagonal cupola, one of the few left in Worcester. Pierced aprons in the gables and dormers in every elevation, bargeboards, gabled window caps, an original entry porch with a pierced brackets bay window, and a panelling

John Hastings Cottage
116-L-5

of strapwork around the base of the first storey mark a few of the many unusual details. Along the property's William Street frontage is a low, "cast-stone" wall which may date from 1880. The cottage was first occupied by John Hastings, a successful grocer who owned the house into the twentieth century.

Joseph Davis House (1884)
41 Elm Street
Peabody & Stearns (Boston)

Designed by the Boston firm of Peabody & Stearns and built in 1884, the Joseph Davis House is one of Worcester's best examples of Shingle Style architecture. The house has an irregular plan with major elevations facing south and west. The south facade has a porch at its first storey, above which at the west end is a bay window surmounted by a steeply pitched, overhanging gable; the east end of the south facade contains the dormered slopes of a two storey gambrel roof. The west elevation is asymmetrical, containing several gables and a central bay window, one wall of which contains a decorative panel bearing the building's construction date. Other features of the house include a tall oriel which lights stair landing, interior and exterior chimneys, and a variety of decorative shingling. Although a new road passes immediately east of the house (where a neighboring house once stood), the Davis House remains in largely original condition, having undergone the partial enclosure of its porch and the removal of the porch railing. The Davis House, which was illustrated in *The Engineering and Building Record* in 1888, was also the subject of extensive interior photographs, showing the original furnishings. The photos are now in the collection of the Worcester Historical Museum. An additional fine detail of the property is its low wall of granite, laid in a broken course, with a rounded coping of brown sandstone.

Joseph Davis, the son of Isaac Davis, was born in Worcester in 1838 and in the 1860s married May Waldo Lincoln, granddaughter of Governor Levi Lincoln. During the 1870s and 1880s the couple lived at 53 West Street until the present house was built on the side lawn of Lincoln's mansion. Davis lived at 41 Elm Street until 1890 when he sold the house to William Rice and moved to Boston. Rice, who

Joseph Davis House
116-L-10

became president of Washburn & Moen Manufacturing Company in 1891, was involved in wire manufacturing from the age of 18 (1852) when he worked as a clerk for Ichabod Washburn & Company. Around 1889 Rice established the wire manufacturing firm of William E. Rice Company in Connecticut, later moving the company to Holyoke, Massachusetts. In 1865 Rice's firm merged with I. Washburn & Moen Company. In 1867 Rice traveled in England where he purchased new rod-rolling equipment which was installed in the Washburn & Moen North Works in 1868–1869 and soon became an important factor in the company's success. During the late 1860s Rice also served as treasurer and general manager of the Quinsigamond Wire Works, which was merged into Washburn & Moen in 1868. In 1877 Rice founded the Worcester Wire Company at South Worcester. In 1899 Rice, who was then president of the Washburn & Moen Manufacturing Company and of the Worcester Wire Company, was instrumental in promoting mergers which led to the formation of the American Steel and Wire Company, later the United States Steel Company. After 1899 William Rice retired from active business. 41 Elm Street remained in the Rice family until 1953 when Albert W. Rice, son of William, gave the property to the Worcester Natural History Society. It now serves as the headquarters of the Worcester Redevelopment Authority.

Katz and Leavitt Apartment House (1926)
53 Elm Street
Lucius Briggs

Designed by Lucius Briggs, and built in 1926 by Isador Katz and Eli Leavitt, the apartment house at 53 Elm Street is architecturally unique in Worcester. The building is five storeys high and is faced with buff brick on all elevations, except for the central section of its facade which is faced with ornate glazed tile. Making extensive use of Venetian Gothic precedent, this tile section rises from a pointed arch entry. Above windows of the third, fourth and fifth storeys are panels containing a variety of Gothic motifs (quatrefoils, pointed arches, crockets and finials) executed in various colors of glazed tiles. At the roof line are pointed-arch balustrades set between sections of brick parapet. Unaltered, #53 has its original

Katz and Leavitt Apartment House
116-L-11

cast-stone stoop and retaining wall. Local tradition states that the building's tiles were imported from Europe, although there is no evidence to support or disprove this assertion.

Lucius Briggs was Worcester's leading architect between 1900–1930. Among Briggs' best public buildings were the former Carbarn and the Memorial Auditorium at Lincoln Square. #53 is the most flamboyant of Briggs' designs and illustrates the strong taste for revivalist styles which existed during the 1920s.

William Hogg House (1897)
54 Elm Street
Fuller & Delano

William Hogg House
116-L-12

Built on the site of an earlier Victorian house (ca. 1860–1870), the William Hogg House was built in 1897, reportedly incorporating just enough of the earlier house to qualify as a renovation, thus avoiding the zoning requirement of brick construction for all new houses in the area. The Hogg House was illustrated in "*Worcester of 1898*," in which it was noted that "during the past year William James Hogg has completed and now occupies the residence at the corner of Elm and Ashland Streets, one of the most beautiful houses in that neighborhood." At present the Hogg House is virtually unaltered from its 1897 Colonial Revival design by Fuller and Delano. The facade is symmetrical with a center entry set behind a Corinthian porch and flanked by bay windows. The east elevation contains a porte cochère supported by Corinthian columns, bay windows, arched windows set in rectangular surrounds (1st storey), and windows with architrave and moulded caps (2nd storey). The house rests on a granite foundation and rises to a slate-covered hip roof with pedimented dormers. Except for the removal of a balustrade at the roof and from the porte cochère, the Hogg House retains all of its Colonial Revival style decorative details.

William James Hogg (1851–1929) was born in Philadelphia and came to Worcester in 1879 when he and his father bought the Crompton Carpet Company in South Worcester. Hogg's grandfather, a native of Scotland, had introduced the manufacture of carpets into the United States in 1831, after which three generations of the family (including Hogg's son) followed the business. In 1884 William J. Hogg and his father acquired the Packachoag Worsted Mills, followed in 1887 by the purchase of the Stoneville Mills in Auburn, Massachusetts. Between 1901 and 1905 Hogg sold his interest in the Worcester Carpet Company (his family's business) to Matthew J. Whittall.

Alexander Marsh House (ca. 1848)
57 Elm Street

Alexander Marsh House
116-L-37

The Alexander Marsh House (ca. 1848) is an unaltered example of the side-hall type of Greek Revival house which enjoyed widespread popularity in Worcester during the 1840s and early 1850s. The house rests on a foundation of rock-faced granite and has corner pilasters, a pedimented gable on its facade and a Doric porch. The main entry has a four-panel wooden door (with jigsaw decoration perhaps added ca. 1860) set between side lights. East of the entry, the facade has two floor to ceiling windows of 6/9 sash; elsewhere the house has 6/6 sash. Of the houses built by Governor Levi Lincoln in his first efforts to develop his Elm Street estate in the 1830s and 1840s, only the Alexander Marsh House remains unaltered on its original site.

In October 1848, Levi Lincoln sold 57 Elm Street to Alexander Marsh of Southborough. At the time of this sale, the property was described as containing "a new dwelling house in the process of completion," which presumably was occupied in 1849. Marsh (1805–1890) came to Worcester as a piano dealer and maintained a store in the American House Block from 1849 to 1858. After 1858 he became a manufacturer of barometers and a "dealer in patent rights" with offices in the Union Block on Main Street. In 1875 Marsh built a brick house at the rear of his original lot (now 2 Oak Street) to which he moved in 1875 or 1876.

After 1875, 57 Elm Street was the home of Henry Alexander Marsh (1836–1914), son of Alexander Marsh. In 1853, Henry Marsh became a clerk at the Central Bank (of Worcester), rising to president in 1892. He served as Mayor of Worcester from 1892 to 1894 and continued to live at 57 Elm Street until his death in 1914.

Isaac Davis House (ca. 1870)
1 Oak Street
Gen. William Walker, Stephen Earle, James Purdon

Isaac Davis House
116-L-13

The Isaac Davis House (1870–1872), now the Worcester Club at 1 Oak Street, is a unique local example of Italianate architecture, resembling the Italianate style in Providence, Rhode Island from which the architect of the house, Gen. William Walker, came. It is constructed of brick, three storeys high with a low hip roof, surrounded by a dentilled and modillioned cornice. The house has symmetrical facades facing Elm and Oak Streets. The Elm Street facade is divided into three bays, with the center one set in a slightly recessed plan of the wall. The center bay now contains a rectangular bay window at the first storey (in place of the original Elm Street entry), surmounted at the second storey by a rectangular window with sandstone architrave and cap on consoles, and at the third storey by an arched window. The outer bays of the facade contain at each storey one set of paired 1/1 windows set in a moulded sandstone architrave with consoles supporting a cap. The Oak Street facade is essentially the same as the Elm Street facade, except that it is larger and has an elaborate Corinthian entry porch, flanked by long windows at its center. Surrounding the house is an exceptionally fine cast-iron fence set into panelled granite posts. Alterations to the house include an 1888 remodelling of the interior (Stephen Earle, architect), the construction of a three storey brick ell in 1911 (James Purdon, architect), and the removal of the original square plan cupola. Built at a cost estimated to have been $100,000, the Davis House is by far the most elaborate of its period extant in Worcester.

Isaac Davis (1799–1883) was a native of Northborough, Massachusetts. After attending Leicester and Lancaster Academies, Davis entered Brown University, graduating in 1822. In late 1822 or 1823 Davis began to study law in the Worcester office of his uncle John Davis and Levi Lincoln (both of whom later became governors of Massachusetts). Admitted to the bar in 1825, Isaac Davis apparently rejected the advice of his uncle that he begin practice in a small country town and opened a law office in Worcester. From the outset, Davis enjoyed a great success in his profession, gradually branching out to become involved in local real estate, business and politics. He was president of Quinsigamond Bank, State Mutual Life

Assurance Company, and the Merchants and Farmers Fire Insurance Company. In addition Davis served as a director of the Worcester & Nashua and the Providence and Worcester railroads.

Active in the local Democratic party, Isaac Davis ran frequently (often unsuccessfully) for state senator and other elective offices despite the local and statewide dominance of the Republican party. He was elected state senator in 1843 and 1854, and mayor of Worcester in 1856, 1858 and 1861. Between 1828 and 1860, Davis was a representative to every national Democratic convention.

Following Davis's death in 1883, the property was sold to the Worcester Club which had been formed in March 1878. Additions for club purposes have been made to the rear of the Davis House, and interior rearrangement of rooms was carried out to adapt for use as a private club.

Charles Allen House (ca. 1855–63)
65 Elm Street

Charles Allen House
116-L-14

The Charles Allen House (1870) is a unique example of Second Empire architecture, consisting of a square-plan main house with an ell centered on its rear wall. The facade contains a slightly projecting central pavilion which is trimmed with quoins and rises to a modillioned cornice and low pediment. Flanking the pavilion at both storeys are paired windows set in single capped frames. The roof of the main block is a convexly curved mansard with original hexagonal pattern slates, panelled railing and incised decoration on its trim. In 1915, Colonial Revival style details (fanlighted main entry, Palladian window in central pavilion, Tuscan entry porch and terrace balustrade) were added to the house along with a one storey library addition on the building's east wall. The house remains unaltered since these additions were carried out.

The Allen House is the second building to occupy this site. The first was a side-hall Greek Revival style house which was built for former Governor Levi Lincoln and sold to Charles Allen in 1854. Having been moved to make way for the present structure, this first house now stands at 39 West Street. Charles Allen (1797-ca. 1869) was a Worcester native who withdrew from Yale University to study law with Samuel Burnside of Worcester. In 1818 Allen was admitted to the bar and from 1818 to 1824 practiced law in New Braintree. In 1824 Allen practiced law in Worcester with John Davis (later a governor of Massachusetts). After 1831 Allen carried on a private practice and pursued an interest in politics. In 1829, 1833 and 1834 Allen was elected representative from Worcester to the Massachusetts General Court; in 1835, 1836 and 1855–1857 Allen served as a state senator. Between 1842 and 1844 Allen was a local judge. In 1860, he was appointed Chief Justice of the newly organized Superior Court of Massachusetts and later was offered a seat in the United States Supreme Court, which he refused. Allen also served as a United States Representative in 1849 and 1853 and was a founder of the national Republican Party in the mid-1850s.

Francis Dewey House (1912)
71 Elm Street
Little & Brown (Boston)

Francis Dewey House
116-L-15

   The Francis Dewey House (1912) is a two and one half storey frame house covered with stucco. Asymmetrical in plan and elevation, the Dewey House was built on the site of a ca. 1860 house, portions of which (particularly the foundation) may have been incorporated into the present structure. Major features are its Flemish gables which contain diamond-pane casements. The entry porch is made of fine cast-stone forming Tuscan columns, an entablature with triglyphs, and balustrade. Except for the replacement of windows, the Dewey House is in original condition.
   Designed by Little & Brown, the Dewey House was one of three different designs for a house presented to Francis Dewey by the firm. Water color renderings show the other two proposals as being similar in scale to the present house, but of different styles, one being Colonial Revival, the other an English Tudor design. The high quality of the design selected, and its nearly unaltered condition, mark it as an important example of the flamboyant "Period" which was popular between 1910 and 1930.
   Francis Dewey (1856–1933) was a native of Worcester and the fourth

generation of his family to serve as a judge. Dewey, in addition to his law practice, had extensive property and business interests in Worcester. From 1898 until his death he was president of the Worcester Consolidated Railway. Dewey was also president of the Norwich & Worcester and the New London Northern Railroad Companies. He served as a trustee of the Worcester Mechanics Savings Bank, Clark University, and a large number of businesses and charitable organizations.

Harris-Merrick House (ca. 1832–44)
41 Fruit Street

Harris-Merrick House
130-L-35

The Harris-Merrick House is a two storey, side-hall plan Greek Revival style house. The corner pilasters are trimmed with simple wooden frets. At the facade are floor-to-ceiling windows and an original entry with side lights. Alterations to the house are limited to the rebuilding of its porch.

It is one of the earliest houses remaining from the initial development of the west side of Worcester which began in the early 1830s when Governor Levi Lincoln subdivided a tract of land known as the Sever Farm. Originally located at 11 Chestnut Street, this house stood among a large number of Greek Revival style residences designed by Elias Carter for the city's leading lawyers and merchants of the 1830s. The Harris-Merrick House was either built for Clarendon Harris, a book seller and first secretary of the State Mutual Life Assurance Company who bought the Chestnut Street lot in 1832; or for Pliney Merrick, a judge and one of the city's most prominent attorneys, who owned the property by 1844. Merrick's first home stood immediately south of the original lot of the Harris-Merrick House, designed for Merrick by Elias Carter in 1831.

Between 1845 and 1847, the Harris-Merrick House was owned and occupied by Frederick W. Gale, an attorney. In 1857 it was sold to Henry Clarke, a physician, who occupied it until 1874 when, planning to build a large stone house on the Chestnut Street lot, he sold the structure to Edward W. Lincoln who moved it to its present site. At the time of the move, the Harris-Merrick House was the only one in the vicinity of Fruit Street, then an open tract which Lincoln was planning to develop. Once on its new site, the building was converted to a two-family house. In the late 1870s Lincoln began active development of the surrounding area, building a number of rental houses. At present the Harris-Merrick House retains most of its original Greek Revival style features and has associations to two stages of the city's westward residential expansion in the nineteenth century.

Merrill Double House (1879)
18–20 West Street

In unaltered condition, the Merrill Double House (ca. 1879) typifies the best of local Victorian Gothic architecture. The house is two and one half storeys high, of brick construction, and is arranged symmetrically about the center party wall. The facade has paired entries at its center, an entry porch supported by columns with stylized foliate capitals, bay windows flanking the entries, steep gables with bargeboards and jerkin head dormers. On both side elevations are rectangular plan bays which rise to a wood-sheathed third storey and steeply pitched roofs with jerkin head gables. An extremely unusual detail of the house is its "cast-stone" (concrete) trim which consists of window lintels, sills and foundation facings. Although Worcester manufacturers are known to have been making "cast-stone" (concrete) trim in the 1870s, the Merrill House is the earliest building with concrete trim to have been identified.

The house was first occupied in 1879 by William A. Denholm (#18), a dry-goods merchant, who founded the Boston Store in 1879, a business which later became the city's largest department store. In 1881, #20 West Street was occupied by Frederick Clark, a provisioner. #18–20 West Street was apparently built as an investment by the heirs of Enoch Merrill, a variety store owner who had built his own home on this site in the 1840s. In plan and detail the Merrill Double House resembles several other double houses built on the West Side during the early 1880s, although no architect has been identified for any of them.

Merrill Double House
116-L-32

Robinson and Swan Blocks
130-E

Robinson and Swan Blocks
104–108 Pleasant Street
1–3 Irving Street
Fuller & Delano

The Robinson & Swan Blocks are three storey brick blocks of nearly identical design joined at the corner of Pleasant and Irving Streets. The major difference between the two attached structures is that the Robinson Block (104–108 Pleasant Street) has a center entry flanked by two storefronts at the first storey, as originally planned, while the Swan Block (1–3 Irving Street) has a center entry flanked by two windows on each side, as originally planned. Otherwise the buildings are virtually identical, with symmetrical facades arranged about a shallow central pavilion. Second storey windows have decorated stone lintels on channeled consoles, while third storey windows have low arched heads framed by stone voussoirs and keystones. Bands of decorative brickwork and dressed stone extend around the buildings at various heights. Especially fine is the arched entry of 1–3 Irving Street, which has polished granite columns, carved stone panels, and stone brackets supporting a shallow balcony and original iron railing. Excepting the modernization of storefronts in the early twentieth century, the Swan & Robinson Blocks are unaltered.

Built in 1884 and designed by the prominent Worcester firm of Fuller & Delano, the Swan and Robinson Blocks occupy a lot which previously contained the wood-frame house of George Swan. It is likely that Swan built both structures and that he sold 104–108 Pleasant Street to Joseph Robinson, a physician, in 1885. After 1885, Swan maintained his law office and residence at 1–3 Irving Street and Robinson maintained his residence and medical office at 104–108 Pleasant Street, a pattern of use which was characteristic of much residential development immediately west of the business district.

Horatio Tower House (1850)
71 Pleasant Street

Horatio Tower House
130-D

One of the best examples of Italianate architecture in Worcester, the Horatio Tower House is a two storey frame structure, set on a rock-faced granite foundation, enclosed by a low, hip roof. The building is nearly square in plan with a small one storey bay centered on its east wall. The facade is symmetrical with a center entry and fanlight, Corinthian porch, oversized first storey windows, window caps on carved consoles, corner pilasters and entablature/cornice with dentils and modillions. East and north elevations are finished with similar details. In contrast to the more flamboyant stucco-covered Italianate villas of the 1850s, the Horatio Tower House is more academic in its use of classical detail. In addition, the plan and pilasters retain elements of local Greek Revival architecture, particularly the many hip-roofed houses designed by Elias Carter between 1829 and 1845. Of the large number of Greek Revival and Italianate style mansions built along Pleasant, Chestnut and Elm Streets during the West Side's early development (1830s–1850s), the Tower House alone remains intact.

The first owner and occupant until 1881, Horatio Tower was a prominent local builder. Around 1824, Tower worked as an apprentice to Captain Lewis Bigelow during the construction of the old town hall. In 1827, Tower worked with Zenas Studley in constructing an addition to the First Baptist Society Church on Salem Street (now demolished). Additional buildings constructed by Tower with partners included Antiquarian Hall, the Old Court House, the Depot of the Boston and Worcester Railroad on Front Street (1835), and the B. & W. Railroad's first engine house (with Tilley Raymond and S. D. Harding). All of the foregoing have since been demolished. The best known building constructed by Tower is Mechanics Hall, of which he was superintendent in the early 1850s. According to the obituary of Tower's wife, the house at 71 Pleasant Street was built by Tower, although the building's architect is not mentioned.

A brick addition was added about 1911 when the building was converted to a funeral home by George Sessions & Sons Company. The property is now owned and occupied by the Junior League of Worcester.

Bull Mansion (G.A.R. Hall—1876)
55 Pearl Street
Calvert Vaux, Stephen Earle

Situated in a commercial area of parking lots and non-descript twentieth century buildings, the Bull Mansion was built in 1876. It is significant architecturally as it was designed by Calvert Vaux, historically in its relationship to the Wessons (an important family in Worcester), and as a vestige of a former period of opulence and craftsmanship.

Constructed as a professional residence for Dr. George Bull and his wife Sarah at a cost of $125,000, the house was the gift of Daniel B. Wesson, father of Sarah. Wesson had made his fortune in the gun manufacturing business. The house proved too expensive for a young doctor to maintain, so Dr. Bull soon found his wife and his residence unsatisfactory. In 1882 he separated from both to go west.

No tenants could be found, and in 1889 the house was sold to Helen M. A. Marble, wife of Dr. John O. Marble. As an interesting coincidence, Helen Marble was the daughter of Ethan Allen who also made his fortune in gun manufacturing. In 1903 the house was sold again to Warren D. Hobbs of Boston. Hobbs gave use of the house to his daughter and her husband, Dr. Howard Beal. Following the departure of the Beals in 1913, the home was sold to the George H. Ward Post 10 of the Grand Army of the Republic (G.A.R.).

The house steadily lost value, and the G.A.R. was able to purchase the building for its assessed value of $21,600. In 1922–1923 a campaign was initiated to raise funds for the construction of an addition to the rear of the building. The addition houses a meeting hall and museum.

As the twentieth century progressed and the members aged, the membership of the G.A.R. post steadily dwindled. What had once been the largest G.A.R. post in the country could soon only boast of a few members. In 1931–1932 the trustees found the expense too great to carry on and the Hall was deeded to the City of Worcester with a number of stipulations attached. The city maintains the building for the use of patriotic groups.

A high Victorian Stick structure of random ashlar Connecticut granite with smooth-faced, light grey granite trim, the Bull Mansion (G.A.R. Hall) is set back

Bull Mansion (G.A.R. Hall)
130-A

from the street with an elaborate fence bordering the sidewalk. Pearl Street slopes downward from west to east. This geographical feature results in a basement level originally used for the professional offices of the owner.

The structure is two and one half storeys high with the third floor partially obscured by the steeply sloped slate roof. A flight of ten steps on the right side of the northern facade leads to the front door. The double doors are protected by a shallow stone porch embellished with carving, polished granite columnettes and ornamental iron-work forming a railing on top. Over the doorway is a granite lintel with the carving, "Post 10 G.A.R." Calvert Vaux, the architect, balanced the facade with an impressive sculptured doorway to one side and a large tower to the other. The steeply pitched slate tower originally had iron cresting and is placed behind one of the two symmetrical gables on the north facade. These large gables have ornamental truss and bargeboard woodwork.

The 1920 addition to the southeast is of slightly different style but uses the same stone. The stone on the side facing Pearl Street was taken from a portion of the fence. The other three walls of the addition are of yellow brick. The architect for the addition was Stephen Earle, and the builder was O. W. Norcross, both of Worcester.

The basement level originally housed the medical offices of the owners. Massive doors of black walnut and mahogany with heavy trim were installed throughout the house. The windows had inside blinds which are still in place today. Ebony and oak were also used for decorative effect in the panelling. The dark woodwork is heavy and used extensively throughout the house. Large mirrors and elaborate gas fixtures have always been considered as important assets and are mentioned as integral parts of the house in the deeds.

The only exterior alterations to the mansion have been the addition to the rear, and the removal of some cast iron ornamentation.

The Boynton and the Windsor
718 and 720 Main Street
Barker & Nourse

The Boynton (718 Main Street) and the Windsor (720 Main Street) are free-standing brick apartment houses of identical design. Of the two buildings, the Boynton remains unaltered. It is four storeys high with a flat roof and a facade that is symmetrically arranged (except for the front door which is south of center) and consists of a wide central bay framed by piers and flanked by narrower outer bays. At the roof line is a panelled brick parapet with a raised central section. At the first storey of the facade is an open entry porch consisting of five arches (three on the front, one on each end) above which are terra cotta tiles and an iron railing. Window trim and copings are of rock-faced sandstone. While the Windsor was originally identical to the Boynton, it now differs by the loss of its parapet and the replacement of its original 1/1 wooden sash with 1/1 metal-frame sash.

Built in 1887 at a cost of $16,000 for J. C. Ellis, a real estate developer, the Boynton was designed by the local firm of Barker & Nourse. Although no building notice has been found for the Windsor, the building's design and construction date (1887–1888) make it likely that it, too, was designed by Barker & Nourse. In their present condition, these two buildings are good examples of local apartment house construction begun in the early and mid-1880s. Also characteristic of early apartment house development in Worcester is the building's original appeal to middle-class tenants. Among the Boynton's earliest tenants were its owner, J. C. Ellis, a physician, a printer, a dressmaker, a hairdresser and two widows. The first tenants of the Windsor included a teacher, an artist, a machinist, an ammunition maker, a clerk, a druggist and Mrs. L. B. Smith, an "electric and botanic physician" who kept an office in her apartment. Prior to recent demolitions, the Boynton and the Windsor were part of the city's most extensive early apartment house district, one which extended along Main Street South, Wellington Street, and northward to Chandler Street. Now fragmented, the architectural types which dominated this area's development during the 1880s and 1890s are best represented by the Boynton, the Windsor, and a cluster of brick apartment houses remaining on Wellington Street.

The Boynton
142-T-3

Moody Shattuck House
141-E

Moody Shattuck House (1885)
768 Main Street
Fuller & Delano

The Moody Shattuck House is an exceptional local example of Queen Anne architecture. Designed by the prominent Worcester firm of Fuller and Delano, the Shattuck House displays unusual familiarity with English Queen Anne design. Its two and one half storey asymmetrical facade contains especially fine details in its moulded brick, sandstone quoining, broken scroll pediment, pilastered window surround, decorative terra cotta panel with a shield inscribed "S," and dormer with its high gable. Decoration continues around to the side walls with pilastered chimneys, dormers with high gables and decorative paneling on exterior chimneys. At the facade is a one storey wooden porch supported by paired columns. Access to the porch is gained through an entry bay surmounted by a low pediment with plaster foliate decoration. Except for the demolition of an original carriage house at its southwest corner, the house is unaltered.

The Shattuck House was built at a cost of $12,000 in 1885 for Moody Shattuck (1835–1892), a cigar manufacturer. A native of Vermont, Shattuck came to Worcester in 1858 and bought a small cigar business soon after his arrival. In 1860 he moved his business to the Walker Building from which it was moved to Clark's Block in 1880. In 1886 Shattuck took John H. Dally and J. A. Clemence as partners in the firm, which was incorporated as M. E. Shattuck Cigar and Tobacco Company in 1888, reputedly the largest business of its type in New England. After Shattuck's death his widow continued to live at 768 Main Street. Although no longer used as a residence, the Shattuck House retains the appearance of a single-family house. It is among the best examples of the free-standing Victorian houses which were built along Main Street South by Worcester industrialists during the last half of the nineteenth century.

Dowley-Taylor Mansion (1842)
770 Main Street
Elias Carter

Dowley-Taylor Mansion
141-F

The Dowley-Taylor mansion (1842) is the best preserved example of the large number of elaborate Greek Revival style houses built in Worcester between the late 1820s and the end of the 1840s. Designed by Elias Carter, few of these handsome buildings remain.

Characteristic of Carter's Worcester designs, this house is a two storey frame structure with a two storey Corinthian portico along its east facade facing the street, plus hip roof and cupola. The facade is symmetrical with the center entry flanked by two floor to ceiling windows with molded caps set on acanthus brackets. The second storey contains five symmetrically spaced windows each with a cap identical to the first storey window caps. The corners of the house are trimmed with pilasters which rise to acanthus and lotus capitals. The cupola is an octagonal structure all enclosed with 6/6 windows bearing original stained glass and surrounded by a circular porch supported by columns with more lotus and acanthus capitals. Alterations have included the removal of the parapet with a carved eagle over the entry and the replacement of sash about 1900.

In his *Greek Revival Architecture in America*, Talbot Hamlin has this to say: "Worcester is especially rich in the work of Elias Carter (1781–1864), a typical example of the New England builder-architect who changed over from an earlier devotion to the refined Late Colonial to a full understanding of Greek Revival. . . It was not until he settled in Worcester in 1828 that his full talent was revealed. He did an enormous amount of work there—churches, business blocks, and houses; it is by the last that he is best known. His houses are large in scale, dignified and simple in mass, and wherever he could he used a two storey colonnade of Greek Doric or Ionic columns extending the full length of the house. Some people, because of these columns have sought to find in them a southern influence. In reality, these Worcester examples frequently pre-date many of the southern mansions. It is therefore probable that their use by Carter was a completely independent invention."

Other Carter houses in Worcester included: the Daniel Waldo house (1830), the

Levi Lincoln house (1836), the Simeon Burt house (1834), the Stephen Salisbury house (1836–1838), the Butman-Sargent house (1829). Of these mentioned, only the Dowley-Taylor, Stephen Salisbury, and Butman-Sargent houses are left. The latter has been greatly altered.

About 1840 Levi Dowley, a shoe and leather merchant who had run a store on the east side of Main Street near Pleasant, decided to build himself a handsome house in keeping with his neighbors, Isaac Davis and Ira Barton. This he did on the site of the present Shawmut Worcester County Bank at 446 Main Street opposite today's City Hall. In 1847 Mr. Dowley suffered financial reverses and sold his lovely house to Ethan Allen, the gun manufacturer. Realizing the growing commercial value of the site, Mr. Allen in 1853 sold the land and moved the house to its present location at 770 Main Street.

Sometime later the Grout family lived in this house. Jonathan was a local bookseller and his son, Willie, was the first Worcester casualty in the Civil War. This is the same Lt. Willie Grout whose heroism at the battle of Ball's Bluff was immortalized by Henry S. Washburn's poem "The Vacant Chair." Later Calvin Taft whose wife was the aunt of Harriette Forbes, became the owner. Dr. Frank Kelley, a mayor of Worcester, bought the house from the Tafts and then sold it to Ransom C. Taylor in 1882. The Taylor family occupied the house for seventy years. The Central New England College is the present owner.

Daniel Stevens House (ca. 1870)
7 Sycamore Street

The Daniel Stevens House is a two storey brick structure with a third storey beneath a slate-covered mansard roof. It has a symmetrical facade consisting of a center entry and open porch (posts were replaced in the 20th century) flanked by three-sided bay windows. Decorative trim consists of quoins, sandstone window lintels with incised decoration, decorative brickwork beneath the cornice, brackets and dormers with brackets. Along the property's frontage is a retaining wall and gate posts, all of dressed granite.

Daniel Stevens (1818–1888) was a native of Charlton, Massachusetts who

Daniel Stevens House
142-A-1

traveled to California with his brother, Charles P., in 1850 in search of gold. By 1853 the two had returned to Worcester where they formed a partnership as D. and C. P. Stevens, painters. In 1854, the Stevens brothers expanded their business to include the manufacture of sash, doors and blinds. Having occupied a building on the site of the present Federal Building (Main and Southbridge Streets), the two Stevens moved their business in 1867 to 32 Southbridge Street, a building which they owned and expanded into a major commercial block. Later they became involved in a variety of ventures including a large grain and flour business, and real estate development along Southbridge Street.

Beginning in 1853, Daniel and Charles Stevens shared a house at 7 Sycamore Street. It is likely that the present house was built around 1865–1870 and that the previous building was either moved to a new location or destroyed. In 1880 Charles Stevens moved to Woodland Street, after which 7 Sycamore Street was occupied by Daniel Stevens.

S. D. Newton House (ca. 1849)
8 Sycamore Street

The S. D. Newton House at 8 Sycamore Street is a fine example of what was the most popular Greek Revival type of house in Worcester during the late 1840s and 1850s—a decade when the population nearly doubled from 11,555 (1845) to 22,285 (1855). Correspondingly, the number of buildings in the city doubled during that same period. Characteristic of the type, the Newton House (built ca. 1849) has a side-hall floor plan, pedimented gable, corner pilasters, side lighted entry, and Doric porch with four columns. Built for S. D. Newton, a house painter, the building's occupants after 1854 were Benjamin Lewis, a victualler at Spurr and Lewis on Main Street, and James Lewis who worked in the telegraph office.

S.D. Newton House
142-A-2

Charles H. Fitch House
141-N

Charles H. Fitch House (1878)
15 Oread Street

First occupied in 1878, 15 Oread Street is an unusual example of Victorian architecture. Its two and one half storey height with narrow windows beneath the eaves, hip roof, deep brackets and double bow front are reminiscent of Italianate style houses built in Worcester during the 1850s. However, rock-faced sandstone foundation, stone banding, decorative brick-banding, central gable with balcony, and open entry porch with jig-saw railing and grilles are more characteristic of local Victorian Gothic architecture. In addition to many fine details, the property possesses a retaining wall, gateposts and steps of dressed granite along its Oread Street frontage.

Charles Fitch, who lived here from 1878 until his death in the early twentieth century, was a boot manufacturer who, in 1850, became a principal in the firm of Otis, Fitch and Company. Shortly after the formation of this firm, Benjamin Otis retired and the company was renamed Fitch and Otis. From 1863 to 1866, the firm was known as Dike and Fitch; later names were C. H. Fitch and Company (1866–1886) and Fitch, Cox and Staple. Characteristic of Worcester's boot and shoe industry which reached its peak in the 1870s and 1880s, Fitch manufactured heavy grades of work boots at his Mulberry Street Factory.

Located in the vicinity of Main Street South, an area which, in the 1970s, experienced widespread abandonment and demolition of former houses, the Fitch House is a rare reminder of the area's Victorian development with the names of many of Worcester's manufacturers.

Edward Stark House (1883)
21 Oread Street
J. B. Woodworth

Resembling the plan of the nearby Norcross Brothers' Houses, the Edward Stark House is an early example of Queen Anne style architecture. The house is two and one half storeys high, rising from a foundation of rock-faced sandstone.

Upper storeys are built of pressed brick with dressed sandstone trim. Major features of the assymetrical facade are a rounded bay which rises to corbelling, a gabled dormer and turret; a porch with turned posts, double front doors, gable with decorative brickwork and chamfered sandstone window lintels. In addition the property retains its original granite stoops and retaining wall along Oread Street. At present the Stark House is unaltered and, together with its neighbor (the Charles Fitch House), serves as a rare reminder of the appearance of the Oread Street neighborhood when it was the home of many of the city's manufacturers during the late nineteenth century.

Edward Stark (1829–1900) was a native of Halifax, Vermont who came to Worcester in 1850. In 1865 he and his brother, O. N., formed a partnership as E. H. Stark & Co., boot and shoe manufacturers. Although Stark is not listed at 21 Oread Street in local directories until 1884, a building notice for the house was published in 1880. This notice gave the estimated cost as $15,000 and names J. B. Woodworth as both architect and builder. Little is known of Woodworth except that he practiced architecture in Worcester from 1877 until his death in 1893. The largest number of Woodworth's known designs are simple cottages and three storey apartment blocks, none of which equal the high quality of the Stark House.

Edward Stark House
141-O

James Scofield House (1860)
3 Mount Pleasant Street

Built around 1860, the Scofield House is an early example of Second Empire style architecture. As with other early houses of its style, the Scofield House has a square floor plan with rear ell. The facade is symmetrical, possessing corner quoins, an original entry porch, side-lighted entry, moulded window caps with dentils and a deep dentilled cornice. Above the cornice is a low, concavely curved mansard roof with two dormers at the facade. At present the house is unaltered.

James Scofield (1824–1871) was a native of Connecticut. From 1845 to 1849 he owned a New London newspaper which he sold upon moving to Stockton, California in 1849. Serving as collector of the port of Stockton, Scofield also sold miners' supplies and attempted to establish a newspaper there, although his

James Schofield House
141-V

printing presses were lost in shipping. About 1855–1857 Scofield returned to the east coast, and in 1865 moved to Worcester to work as an agent for the Charter Oak Life Insurance Company of Hartford, Connecticut. During his six years in Worcester before his death, Scofield developed an extensive insurance business employing agents through the state. At the same time, Scofield purchased large tracts of open land along Main Street South and tried to promote zoning which would have required that all new houses along Main Street be set 150 feet back from the street. Intending that Main Street become a "grand avenue," Scofield succeeded in persuading some individual owners to follow this proposed restriction. However, his death in 1871 brought an end to the planned development of Main Street South.

"Brightside" (1889)
2 King Street
Fuller & Delano

"Brightside"
141-Z

"Brightside" is one of several dozen, red brick, Romanesque Revival style apartment houses built in the Main-South area during the 1880s and 1890s. Of its period, Brightside is one of the more elaborate and better preserved. Among the most expensive of its type, it cost $40,000 to build in 1888. In addition to its carved Romanesque style details in sandstone, the facade is heavily ornamented with large terracotta panels of stylized floral decoration. This building's unique ornamentation indicates that the architects prepared the design to order, unlike later apartment houses which appear to have been built according to several standardized plans. The building was renovated after a 1977 fire. It was renovated again and enlarged in 1983–1984.

Lucius Knowles House (1870)
838 Main Street

Lucius Knowles House
141-J

The main body of the Lucius Knowles House was built in 1870 and remains among the city's best examples of Second Empire architecture despite the application of aluminum siding. The facade is symmetrical containing a slightly projecting pavilion at its center. At the first storey this pavilion contains two pairs of ornate wooden doors and an original entry porch. On the south elevation is a second original porch (now glazed) above which a semi-circle oriel has been added (ca. 1900). Other details of the building's original design are its concavely curved mansard roof covered with fish-scale slates and paired cornice brackets which have carved swags at their bases.

A unique detail of the Knowles House is its music room which was designed by Stephen Earle of Worcester and added to the northeast corner. This bay was reputedly designed to provide space for a harp played by Knowles's daughter. Both the skylights, set in a coved ceiling, are now covered on the exterior but intact and visible on the interior. The room's interior was decorated with wooden panelling, varying bands of arabesques (in plaster or lincrusta) and stained glass windows bearing portraits of musicians and artists. The Knowles House music room was one of the most important Victorian interiors in Worcester, one which represents the most advanced taste of its period. Other rooms in the house contain a variety of Second Empire and Colonial Revival style fittings.

Lucius Knowles (1819–1884) was a native of Hardwick, Massachusetts who pursued a variety of businesses before achieving prominence as an inventor and manufacturer of looms. By 1842, Knowles had become Worcester's first daguerreotyper. In 1843, Knowles added electro-gilding and silver plating to his business. Subsequent business ventures of Knowles included the spooling of thread (1844), the manufacture of cotton warp at Spencer (1847) and the manufacture of satinets at Warren (1855–1858). In 1856, Knowles made the first of many improvements in the design of looms for making "fancy goods." By 1862, Knowles and his brother, Frank B., were manufacturing looms for hoop-skirt tapes. In 1863, the brothers took patents on their designs and, in 1866, the firm moved to Worcester.

Once in Worcester, the company's business grew rapidly, based on new inventions of the Knowles brothers, including improved looms for plaids (1868). Known for their use of the open shed principle, the Knowles' took out a patent in 1873 for a broadloom for fancy woolens. In 1876, the brothers added a forty-harness loom which was exhibited at the Centennial Exposition. By 1879, the firm's increasing business led to the rental of large portions of the Junction Shop which was occupied by the Knowles Loom Works until 1890 when the Grand Street Factories were built. In 1897, the Knowles Loom Company was merged with the Crompton Loom Company to form Crompton and Knowles Loom Works.

John Legg House (1896)
5 Claremont Street
Stephen Earle

John Legg House
141-B-1

The John Legg House is an opulent Queen Anne style house, one which remains unaltered except for the application of asbestos shingles over clapboard and wooden shingles. Two and one half storeys high, the house is of frame construction and has asymmetrical plan and elevations. Set above street level, the facade is approached by two flights of granite stairs which lead to the pedimented entry bay of the porch. Major elements of the facade include a three sided bay window with parapet, a gambrel dormer with Palladian window, fanlighted entry, and first and second storey porches. Ornate details appear on all of the house's elevations and include a pedimented oriel window, elaborate stained glass (stair hall) windows and Ionic porches. Extending along the property's Claremont Street frontage is a retaining wall of rock-faced granite ashlar.

John Legg (b. 1851), who occupied the house from 1896 to 1912, was the third generation of his family to be involved in textiles. Legg's grandfather and father, James, had been British weavers. Around 1854 James moved to the United States, settling in Rhode Island. In 1865 he set up his own factory in Burrillville, Rhode Island, where John learned about woolen manufacturing. In 1881 the elder Legg purchased the Worcester Woolen Company located at the Lower Junction Shop on Hermon Street. Reorganized as James & John Legg, the firm produced heavy woolen materials, "cassimeres," and suitings. After the death of James Legg in 1890, a new corporation was formed and John Legg became general manager of the Worcester Mills, a position which he held through subsequent partnerships. Under Legg's management and ownership, the Worcester Woolen Mills Company became one of the city's largest textile producers, employing more than 300 workers in the first two decades of the twentieth century. After 1912, Legg and his family moved to a new house on Lenox Street, the new residential park land laid out on "Chamberlain Hill" in Worcester's west side.

Franklin Wesson House (1874)
8 Claremont Street
A. R. Cutting

First occupied in 1875, architectural historians call the Wesson house "the finest High Victorian Gothic style extant in Worcester." Designed by A. R. Cutting, it is among the few remaining brick buildings of its kind. The house displays a variety of decorative details including a central four storey tower with low-rising, pointed arch entry, buttresses, lancet windows, and dormered high hip roof. Elsewhere the house has belt courses of decorative brick, pointed arch windows with sandstone springers and keystones, fine granite site fittings and granite entry steps. Despite conversion from a single family residence to several apartments, and with the exception of a two storey wooden porch at the northeast corner, the building appears unaltered and an important survivor from Worcester's past.

The house was constructed for Franklin Wesson, a founder of Worcester's arms industry. In 1871 Wesson formed the firm of Wesson and Harrington, later to become the Harrington and Richardson Arms Company, for the manufacture of "a shell-ejecting revolver." By the 1890s, the house was occupied by Charles S. Forbes, an attorney, and in 1911 by F. Thayer, secretary of the A. D. Thayer Company, cloth manufacturers.

Franklin Wesson House
141-B-2

Norcross Brothers Houses (1878–79)
16 and 18 Claremont Street

Shown on the 1878 Map of Worcester, the James and Orlando Norcross Houses are perhaps Worcester's earliest examples of Queen Anne style architecture. Identical in plan and massing, the houses stand as near mirror images of each other. Both buildings are constructed of rock-faced sandstone, laid in a broken course of squared blocks, and are two and one half storeys high with a dormered attic above the top storey. Both houses have asymmetrical facades consisting of a central entry flanked by tripartite windows on one side and a rounded corner bay rising to a dormered turret on the other side. Principal differences between the houses are that the James Norcross House (18 Claremont) retains decorative slate tiling set in a checkered pattern on its gables, and has a porch which terminated in a curved roof supported by a single massive bracket, while the Orlando Norcross House (16 Claremont) has a porch which extends eastward to become a porte cochère. Both buildings share the same arrangement of gables, dormers and chimneys. Interiors of the two houses contain a great variety of wood paneling (mostly original to 1878–1880 and made of oak), stained glass, art tiles and decorated window and door surrounds. The interior of the James Norcross House appears to have been the more elaborate from the beginning, with an especially fine oak-paneled stair-hall. The large corner lot on which the houses stand originally contained a stone stable (now demolished) which the Norcrosses shared.

Built for the nationally famous Norcross Brothers, builders, 16 and 18 Claremont Street were influential in the introduction of the Queen Anne style to Worcester. Soon after the houses were built, buildings of similar plan and elevation began to be designed by such diverse local architects as Stephen Earle and J. B. Woodworth.

The Norcross Brothers (James Atkinson and Orlando W.) were born in Maine in 1831 and 1839 respectively, sons of a carpenter/builder, Jesse Springer Norcross. In 1843 the Norcross family moved to Salem, Massachusetts, near which the brothers founded Norcross Brothers (builders) in 1864 following the return of Orlando Norcross from the Civil War. By 1868 the Norcrosses were settled in Worcester, where in 1869–1870 the firm built the old Worcester High School (now

Norcross Brothers House
18 Claremont
141-B-3

Norcross Brothers House
16 Claremont
141-B-3

demolished) from plans by Henry Hobson Richardson of Boston. This contact seems to have resulted in the Norcross Brothers receiving most of the construction contracts for Richardson's most famous buildings of which Trinity Church, Boston, is the best known. It is thought that the firm and its ingenuity in masonry construction was partially responsible for the development of Richardson's unique Romanesque style, and indirectly for the popularity which heavy masonry achieved during the late nineteenth century. In addition to the Norcross' work for H. H. Richardson, the firm worked with many of the most prominent architects of its day, including McKim, Mead & White; Shepley, Rutan & Coolidge (successors to H. H. Richardson); Peabody & Stearns; and others. Among the many well-known buildings built by the Norcross Brothers are the New York Public Library, the Rhode Island State House, the remodeling of the White House carried out under Theodore Roosevelt, the Allegheny County Courthouse (Pittsburgh) and, in Worcester, the State Mutual Building (340 Main Street) and the Worcester City Hall. The architect of the Norcross Houses is unknown. The firm's contact with many prominent architects, as well as its maintenance of an architectural staff, makes an attribution of design impossible. Nonetheless, the buildings remain as two of the finest of their style in Worcester.

Elias Crawford House (1851)
3 Norwood Street

Elias Crawford House
153-H

Built prior to 1860, the Elias Crawford House is one of two octagonal houses in Worcester. The other is the Richard Barker House at 312 Plantation Street. The Crawford House is a two storey frame structure of the octagonal plan with a service wing on its south and west sides. An open porch supported by chamfered wooden posts with brackets extends around the building's first floor. Its fenestration is irregular and the structure is enclosed by a hipped roof with open eaves and pendant brackets. Built prior to 1860, later alterations to the house include double front doors and some stained glass (ca. 1890). Immediately southwest of the house is a nineteenth century stable which may be original.

Although the Crawford House is shown on an undated map of the 1860s, no owner's name is given until the 1870 city atlas which lists the house as belonging to

Elias B. Crawford, a cotton and woolen manufacturer. It would seem fairly certain, therefore, that the house was built for an earlier owner. A brief biography of Elias Crawford appearing in Charles Nutt's "History of Worcester" suggests that it may have been Crawford's father who owned 3 Norwood Street. In any event, from the 1880s until 1932, the house was the home of Charles R. Johnson, an attorney who for over half a century was one of the best known members of the Worcester County Bar. A member of the Worcester School Committee for 23 years, Johnson was its chairman for most of that period and was said to have exerted great influence on the Worcester school system of that day.

"Fairlawn" (1893)
189 May Street
James A. Norcross

Located on thirty-eight acres of May Street, James A. Norcross designed and built his "Fairlawn" in 1893 of rock-faced, brown sandstone in Romanesque/Queen Anne style. Since 1922 it has been the Fairlawn Hospital. Retaining the broad, sloping lawns for which the property was named, it is the most architecturally and historically significant Victorian "country estate" remaining in Worcester.

The main house, which remains as the central section of the hospital, has outer dimensions of 70' x 125' two and one-half and three storeys high. The exterior contains few stylistic references to the revivalist styles popular in the 1880s. Instead it is dominated by the heaviness of its masonry construction (a Norcross trademark), and idiosyncratic details which seem to serve both for picturesque effect and to take advantage of the views from this hilltop site. Centered on the facade and rear walls are semi-circular pavilions. The facade pavilion is surrounded by a one storey open porch, supported by slender sandstone columns, and is surmounted above the third floor by a domed cupola. At the four corners of the front section are circular bays rising to three storeys and all connected to the main roof by a peculiar shed-roof arrangement. Despite the addition of hospital wings, the original house remains largely unaltered.

James Norcross and his brother Orlando came to Worcester in 1868. Although

"Fairlawn"
121-A-1

their construction firm of Norcross Brothers was well established before their arrival here, its national fame developed later beginning, perhaps, with the construction of Worcester High School in 1869–1870 (now demolished) and Trinity Church, Boston (1873–1877) both designed by Henry Hobson Richardson. Norcross Brothers played a prominent role in the development of Richardson's Romanesque style because of the firm's unique ability with masonry construction.

Arad Alexander House (ca. 1845)
53 Waverly Street

Built about 1845, this is one of the finest, most elaborately ornamented Greek Revival style houses in Worcester. Its high quality Corinthian columns and pilasters, the entry and fine window hoods with carved consoles, bands of tongue and dart, egg and dart moulding, and foliate modillions suggests the design and work to be that of Elias Carter in the 1840s. Unfortunately, no other temple-front houses designed by Carter are known to exist in Worcester eliminating one basis for comparison. The house was moved to its present location in 1867–1868 for Arad Alexander, a "truckman" and owner of Alexander & Martin. The original owner and location are unknown. Whatever the house's origin, it remains in largely unaltered condition, and is an extremely important local example of Greek Revival architecture. Alterations consist of a new front door and wooden shingling, neither of which interferes with the building's best features.

Arad Alexander House
143-J

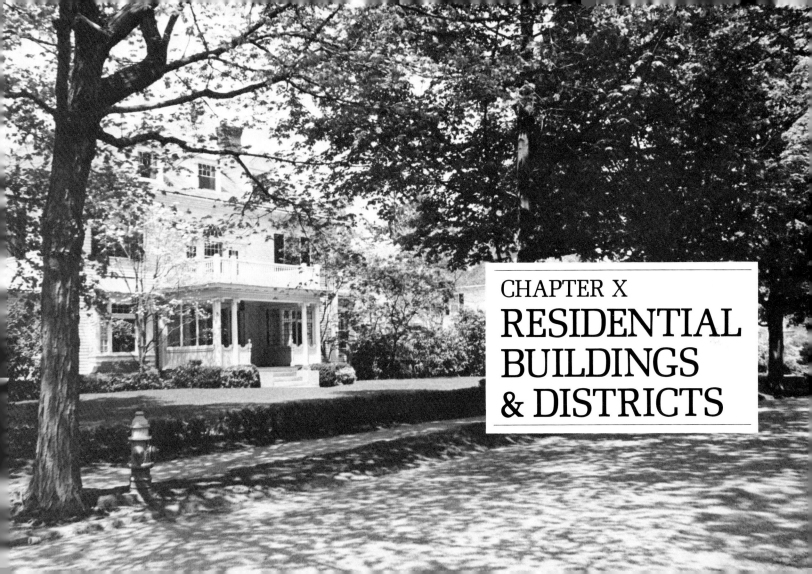

CHAPTER X
RESIDENTIAL BUILDINGS & DISTRICTS

RESIDENTIAL DISTRICTS

With a current population that is approximately 20,000 less than its 1917 population, Worcester has a housing stock, concentrated at its core, which was built mostly before 1917. The largest number of buildings are free-standing frame houses, followed by "three-decker" houses and brick apartment houses. The city's old inner neighborhoods are contained within an irregularly shaped area bounded roughly by Park Avenue, on the west, Salisbury, Belmont, Lincoln and Forestdale Streets on the north, Green Hill Park, Chandler Hill Park, and Interstate 290 on the east and the Middle River between I-290 and Park Avenue on the south. This area was almost completely developed prior to 1900 and contain a variety of building types.

Districts within this area which retain their integrity and are representative of the period include the Oxford-Crown District (and Extension), the Lincoln Estate-Elm Park District, the May Street District and the Woodland Street District. Three later districts exist to the northwest of this core area. These are the Montvale District, the Hammond Heights District, and the Massachusetts Avenue District. One final area, the Indian Hill District, is located far to the north and was constructed by the Norton Company to house its employees.

Individual residences which serve as outstanding examples of particular architectural styles or as characteristic building types associated with important local persons and events have been included here. Districts have been selected for architectural quality and for their ability to demonstrate characteristic patterns of development.

photo on page 203
Massachusetts Avenue District

INDIAN HILL—NORTH VILLAGE DISTRICT
Greendale
Grosvenor Atterbury (New York)

1 and 3 Marconi Road
24-E

Worcester's largest planned community of employee housing, Indian Hill's North Village, was built for Norton Company during WWI. Made up of 94 cottages, it is situated on the north slope of Indian Hill just south of Ararat Street in the Greendale section of North Worcester. Except for the Community Hall (24–26 Watt Road), the Community Store (8–10 Watt Road), and four modern houses (13–21 Heroult Road), all buildings in this district are simple cottages, one and one half storeys high, with steeply pitched, slate-covered roofs. With few exceptions, most of the cottages remain unaltered.

Picturesque, almost "old world" in appearance, these were originally white-walled with grey-green roofs. The result of a corporation wanting to provide good, inexpensive housing in a park-like setting for its workers, all were eventually sold to the company employees at cost.

Plans for the village and its houses were designed by Grosvenor Atterbury of New York. He was also responsible for the South Village (59 cottages) begun and occupied in 1914. Severely altered by recent highway construction, the South Village was not listed in the National Register.

Within the North Village district are buildings of three types:

Type 1 is a one and one half storey cottage with rectangular floor plan symmetrical, center entrance facades, the first storey covered with clapboarding, the second with shingles. Centered on the facades are one-bay entry porches framed by lattice supports and gabled (or shed) roofs with exposed rafters. Windows are 6/6 sash (1st storey), 3/3 sash (between the eaves), and 6/6 sash (2nd storey of gable ends). Cottages of this type account for 89 buildings within the district.

Type 2 consists of two buildings sited as mirror images to each other at 8–10 and 24–26 Watt Road. Nearly identical, each contains a one and one half storey cottage with a long rear ell. The rear wing of 8–10 Watt Road originally contained a Community Store, while that of 24–26 Watt Road contained a Community Hall. Both wings are one storey with gabled end walls, groups of two and three windows

8-10 Watt Road
24-E

with transoms, and asymmetrically placed entries with hoods set on brackets.

Type 3 buildings are one storey ranch houses built after 1960 and do not contribute to the Village's historical significance. They include 13, 17, 19 and 21 Heroult Road.

Historically, Norton Company's efforts are unique in Worcester as company-owned employee housing has been virtually non-existent throughout the City's development with the possible exception of a small number built by Washburn & Moen and Ashworth & Jones.

Ararat Street #101, 109, 111, 113, 115, 117, 129, 131, 133, 135, 137, 139
Delaval Road #3, 5, 6, 7, 8, 9, 10, 11, 13, 14, 15, 16, 17, 18
Heroult Road #5, 7, 8, 9, 10, 11, 12, 16, 18, 22, 23, 24, 25, 26, 29, 30, 32
Marconi Road #1, 3, 5, 7, 12, 13, 14, 15, 16, 23, 24, 25, 26, 27, 28, 29, 30
Watt Road #4, 6, 7, 8–10, 9, 11, 12, 15, 17, 21, 22, 23, 24–26, 25, 27, 28, 30, 31
Westinghouse Road #1, 2, 3, 4, 5, 6, 7, 8, 13, 14, 15, 16

KNOLLWOOD DISTRICT
425 Salisbury Street
Little & Brown (Boston)

The Knollwood District contains 15 acres of the former Lyman Gordon estate of 122 acres. Boundaries for the district include the main house, second house, stable, caretaker cottages, and the open land surrounding these buildings.

Among Worcester's period houses, "Knollwood" is perhaps the grandest. Commissioned by Worcester industrialist Lyman Gordon, a founder of Wyman-Gordon Company, the house was under construction in 1914 when he died. Based on French manor house style of the 17th and 18th centuries, Little & Brown of Boston were the architects of this 20-room residence. The facade consists of a central pavilion with ornamented gable flanked by symmetrical pavilions which form a shallow court around the entry drive. Set back from and flanking this central block are nearly symmetrical wings which terminate in slight pavilions of which the western one has a Palladian motif opening at the first floor. The building is covered by stucco worked to appear as quoining at building corners and at

425 Salisbury Street
75-A

✠
206

window trim. The roof is of green tile. The house possesses beautiful iron work seen in its entry gates, interior stair railings, balconies, door grilles, and an iron and glass marquise.

In addition to the high architectural quality of the main house, the estate retains its original out-buildings which include a second house (of similar design to the main house, but scaled down), three employee cottages, and two former stable/service buildings.

In 1917, "Knollwood" was purchased by Lucius J. Knowles, president of Crompton & Knowles Loom Works. After Mr. Knowles' death, the house was occupied by his widow. In 1928, the estate was sold to Theodore T. Ellis, president of New England Fibre Blanket Company. Since the early 1950s, "Knollwood" has been a girls' school operated by Notre Dame Academy.

Although most of the estate's 122 acres has been subdivided into house lots, and a modern school building constructed southeast of the main house, the immediate surroundings, plantings, and access to Salisbury Street have been left as originally planned. In good condition, the house is a unique, local example of one of the latest and most opulent phases of revivalist architecture.

Salisbury Street #425, 425B, 425C, 425D, 425E, 425F, 425G

425E Salisbury Street
75-A

MASSACHUSETTS AVENUE DISTRICT

The Massachusetts Avenue District runs in a north-south direction for one block between Salisbury Street, which crosses it on the north, and Drury Lane at the south end. A grassy mall thirty feet wide divides the avenue with tall shade trees forming green arches over the street and mall. Lawns lead from the sidewalks to the green shrubbery which surrounds all but one of the eleven residences in the district. These dwellings are evenly spaced along both sides of the street, and, with one exception, are set well back from it.

These impressive houses are examples typical of the fashionable trends and architectural styles of the seventeen-year period (1889–1906) during which they

6 Massachusetts Avenue
88-A

were built. The interest of the era in preservation is illustrated by the Trumbull Mansion built in 1751 as the Second Worcester County Court House. In 1899 this two storey Colonial house, with hipped roof and end chimneys, was moved to its present location and converted to residential use. This house is the focal point of the district because of its situation at the mid-point on the street, and because it is the only example of the late Colonial period here. Its neat, uncluttered lines, low rectangular mass, symmetrical five bay facade, and two storey height are elements which make it typical of this style.

In contrast to the simplicity and dignity of the Trumbull Mansion are its Colonial Revival neighbors. Eight of the eleven houses in the district are built in this style. Although all of these large and elaborately ornamented buildings possess some or most of the stylistic characteristics (the rectangular plan, two and one half storey height, hipped roofs with pedimented dormer windows, one has a gambrel roof, and symmetrical facades), each is individually designed to reflect the taste of the owner and architect. The heavy proportions, deep (and therefore prominent) roofs, the ells and piazzas placed asymmetrically for convenience, as well as the use of large windows and bays, are influences from the Shingle and Queen Anne styles.

There are two exceptions to the Colonial architectural tradition in the district. These face each other across the mall at the south end of the street. The most distinctive features of these houses are their large and decorative half-timbered and stucco gables which are elements typical of the Tudor style. Although this style is visually dominant, influences of the Queen Anne, Shingle and Richardsonian styles are also apparent in one or both of the buildings. #12 Massachusetts Avenue illustrates the Queen Anne and Shingle styles in the deep intersecting gambrelled roofs and the use of shingles as a prominent building material. The first storey of #15 is low and faced with fieldstone which extends as a wall beyond the facade of the house. This creates a horizontality which is accented by the stone lintels covering the windows on this floor. The use of this material and the effect of horizontality when combined with a deep roof recalls some of Richardson's work.

All of the buildings are in excellent condition, and, except for the Trumbull Mansion, retain their original appearances.

Massachusetts Avenue #1, 2, 5, 6, 7, 8, 10, 11, 12, 15
Salisbury Street #201

MONTVALE DISTRICT

Encompassing portions of Monadnock, Sagamore, Whitman, and Waconah Roads, plus two houses on Salisbury Street, the Montvale District contains excellent examples of Queen Anne Colonial Revival and early twentieth century styles of architecture. Prior to 1897, this area was largely undeveloped, containing only the Dresser-Whitman House (246 Salisbury Street), a stable, and outbuildings (now demolished). Built around 1851 for George Dresser, a boot and shoe dealer, the Dresser-Whitman House originally consisted of only its central section, a side hall plan Greek Revival style house with pedimented gable and Doric entry porch. By 1870, the property was bought by Jared Whitman, Jr. who sold it to Ephraim Whitman, a farmer. Around 1897, the property was sold to H. Ballard and M. O. Wheelock, real estate developers, who prepared a subdivision plan for the area creating 73 house lots. Whether Ballard and Wheelock retained the Dresser-Whitman House or sold it immediately is not known.

Houses built on the newly laid out lots included excellent examples of Queen Anne and Colonial Revival styles of architecture, the most notable of which are 254 Salisbury Street illustrated in an 1898 catalogue of the designs of George Clemence; 11 Monadnock Road, the home of Clellan Fisher, a prominent local architect; 12 Monadnock Road, the area's most opulently decorated Queen Anne style house; and 96 Sagamore Road, a good example of Colonial Revival style architecture. Development of the district's eastern half took place slightly later and includes excellent examples of Arts & Crafts/Neo-Tudor architecture (9 & 23 Whitman Road, and 30 Waconah Road) as well as an eclectic, stucco-covered house (22 Whitman Road) with an unusual octagonal pavilion. In addition to the area's well preserved architecture, the plan of its winding, tree-lined streets and hillside site help to preserve the atmosphere and appearance of Montvale's development as an upper-class suburb prior to World War I.

Monadnock Road #2, 11, 12
Sagamore Road #87, 88, 96
Salisbury Street #246, 254
Waconah Road #30
Whitman Road #9, 14, 16, 20, 22, 23, 24, 29, 35, 36

20, 16 Whitman Road
76-C

96 Sagamore Road and
12 Monadnock Road
76-C

HAMMOND HEIGHTS DISTRICT

Hammond Heights is a handsome, well-preserved, suburban neighborhood begun about 1890 covering three blocks of a hillside site between Highland Street and Institute Road. The area includes properties on Westland, Germain, Haviland and Highland Streets, and Institute Road. Prior to 1890, the area was part of the John Hammond Farm, although a subdivision plan had been prepared before 1886 creating Germainia (now Germain) Street, Buffalo (now Haviland) Street, Genesee (now Westland) Street and parts of Sunnyside (later Mt. Hope, now Institute) Road. Between 1890 and 1896, sixteen houses were built along Germain and Highland Streets. By 1911, an additional forty houses appeared along Westland and Haviland Streets. By 1928, the area's last house was completed and Hammond Heights assumed its present appearance.

The area's architecture offers a range of styles and house types which were popular in the middle and upper-middle-class suburbanization of Worcester's West Side at the turn of the century. Most of the area's houses appear to be architect-designed and built for their original owner/occupants, rather than for a real estate developer.

The earliest house in Hammond Heights is the former home of John Hammond (264 Highland Street). One of Worcester's best examples of Italianate architecture, the Hammond House is two storeys high with a low hip roof and a symmetrical center entrance facade. The house has trim of quoins, window hoods on consoles, a cornice with scalloped frieze, and a porch with an octagonal pavilion.

In the 1840s much of the land surrounding the Hammond House was part of a farm which was owned by Governor Levi Lincoln. In the late 1840s the farm, then containing an eighteenth century farmhouse, was sold to John Hammond, a farmer, who occupied the premises together with several members of his family. By 1860, 264 Highland Street had been erected, although it is not clear whether it was built for John or Frederick Hammond. By the 1890s most of the farm land had been sold, and the suburban development of the area began.

The earliest suburban houses in Hammond Heights include several exceptional examples of Queen Anne style architecture, notably 31 Germain Street (illustrated in a book of designs by Barker & Nourse, 1898), 284 Highland Street (an ornately

264 Highland Street
101-B

210

decorated structure) and 26 Germain Street (a two and one half storey "cottage" with corner tower). #17 Germain Street with its pedimented facade, Palladian window and ornate balustrade; 11 Westland Street with hip roof, quoins and a Palladian window; and 26 Haviland Street, which resembles 11 Westland Street, all offer excellent examples of Colonial Revival architecture. Although Queen Anne architecture retained its popularity up to 1910, other contemporary styles are represented including Bungalow style (7 Haviland Street, 8, 20 & 24 Germain Street), and Arts & Crafts/neo-Tudor style (3 Germain Street, 6, 16, & 28 Haviland Street).

Additional houses, such as 28 Westland Street with a stucco base, shingled upper storey and deep eaves show the combined influence of the Arts & Crafts movement and architecture of Chicago's Prairie School. The good condition of most houses in the area, as well as the tree-lined streets, broad unfenced lawns, and hillside site make Hammond Heights one of the most attractive and best examples of Worcester's turn-of-the-century suburbanization.

Germain Street #1, 2, 3, 4, 5, 6, 8, 9, 10, 11, 12, 14, 15, 16, 17, 18, 20, 21, 22, 23, 24, 26, 27, 29, 31
Haviland Street #2, 3, 4, 5, 6, 7, 8, 9-11, 10, 12-14, 15, 16, 17, 19, 20, 21, 22, 23, 26, 28
Highland Street #264, 272, 276, 278, 280-282, 284
Institute Road #161
Westland Street #2, 3, 4-6, 5, 7, 8-10, 9, 11, 12, 13, 14, 15, 17, 18, 19, 20, 21, 22, 23, 24, 25, 26, 27-29, 28, 32, 34, 36

From 15 Westland Street
101-B

LINCOLN ESTATE-ELM PARK DISTRICT

50, 52, 54 Cedar Street
116-L

The Lincoln Estate-Elm Park District is an extensive residential area which contains a large number of architect-designed houses including many of Worcester's best examples of Victorian and early twentieth-century styles. Having enjoyed nearly continuous popularity as an upper-class neighborhood from the late 1840s until the 1930s, the area has many houses associated with Worcester's most prominent businessmen, lawyers and industrialists.

Initial development in the area resulted both from a boom in Worcester's population during the 1840s and the efforts of Governor Levi Lincoln who, in the 1830s, had inherited extensive property along Elm Street. The earliest construction in this general area occurred slightly outside the present district boundaries on Elm Street where Lincoln built a temporary house for himself in 1834. This he replaced with a large mansion in 1836 (now relocated at Old Sturbridge Village). Around 1847–1848 Lincoln built at least four side hall, Greek Revival houses on Elm Street west of his mansion. Originally located outside of the present district bounds, three of these houses were moved into the district in the 1870s when the original lots were rebuilt with larger houses. All three were enlarged and redesigned by local architects, but each retains much of its Greek Revival design. Although Lincoln remained active in the area's development until his death in the late 1860s, most of his efforts were concentrated around Elm Street, leaving large undeveloped parcels along Fruit, William and Sever Streets which would be more actively developed by Lincoln's heirs in the 1880s and 1890s.

From the mid-1850s until the early 1870s, building was concentrated along Cedar Street, east of West Street where houses such as William A. William's early Second Empire style house (26 Cedar Street) represent the most advanced taste of the period. Although many of the buildings of the period were replaced with larger houses in the early twentieth century, important examples of Second Empire and Italianate styles remain at 15 & 20 Cedar Street and at 54 West Street.

After 1869, lots west of West Street were divided between Levi Lincoln's sons, William S., Daniel W., and Edward W. of whom William and Edward took the most active role in the area's development. At Daniel's death in the early 1880s, his property was inherited by his daughter, Frances Merrick Lincoln, who built a large number of architect-designed houses around Fruit Street in the 1880s and around Sever Street in the 1890s. Although Frances Lincoln made use of out-of-town architects (E. C. Gardner of Springfield and W. R. Emerson of Boston), the largest number of houses in the area were designed by local firms, particularly by Stephen Earle, Barker & Nourse, and Fuller & Delano.

In addition to houses built on speculation by the Lincoln family, building lots continued to be sold to increasingly wealthier businessmen and manufacturers. Of the houses built on these lots, the most distinguished are the John Putnam House (23 Fruit Street), a superb example of Stick style architecture; the Charles Davis House (30 Fruit Street) and the Ann Colton House (41 Cedar Street). In the mid-1880s lower Cedar Street (between Russell and Sever Streets) was opened and quickly built up on its north side with an impressive group of Shingle style and Queen Anne style houses (54-62 Cedar Street). In the late 1880s and early 1890s, all remaining lots on Cedar Street were developed. Among the most impressive of this period is "Burns' Folly" (65 Cedar Street), a "chateauesque" and Queen Anne style house which reputedly cost $30,000 to build in 1893. According to local tradition, the expense of building 65 Cedar Street nearly ruined its owner (William Burns, an underwear manufacturer) who was forced to sell it soon after completion. In apparent contradiction to this tradition, Burns built 57 Cedar Street, an elaborate Colonial Revival style house, in 1895.

By the mid-1890s, nearly all lots in the district contained houses, leaving only the Worcester County Agricultural Fair Grounds undeveloped. Bounded by Russell, Highland and Sever Streets and by the back lots of Cedar Street, the Fair Grounds had been bought by the Worcester Agricultural Society. The speed with which lots had been sold on lower Cedar Street encouraged the Society to sell its land to a real estate development company which laid out lower William Street around 1899-1900. However, the concurrent expansion of the city's street railway made rural areas accessible and undercut the demand for lots in more densely built areas. As a result, the north side of lower William Street was not fully built up until 1912, while the south side of the street retained vacant lots until 1927-1929. Exhibiting the same high architectural quality found elsewhere in the district, lower William Street contains excellent examples of the eclectic tastes of the early twentieth century. Particularly distinguished are the Harrower House (#98), the

23 Fruit Street
116-L

64-62, 60 William Street
116-L

15 Oxford Street
130-O

Southgate House (#84), the Higgins House (#80), and the Forbes House (#81).

While lower William Street was being laid out, extensive rebuilding was carried out at the district's east end, on Cedar and Oak Streets, where three Victorian houses were removed and replaced by the elaborate Colonial Revival style houses of William Inman (7 Oak Street) and Ransom F. Taylor (6 Oak Street), and by the Tudor "period" house of Paul B. Morgan (21 Cedar Street). Since World War II, the Lincoln Estate-Elm Park District has become increasingly institutional in use, particularly east of Sever Street where many buildings now serve as offices, dormitories and classrooms. Despite this change in use, the district retains a residential appearance with few intrusions.

Cedar Street #15, 19, 20, 21, 26, 28–32, 34, 35, 36, 38–40, 39, 41, 44, 45, 46, 47–49, 48, 50, 52, 54, 55, 56–58, 57, 60, 61, 62, 64, 65, 67
Fruit Street #23, 30, 37, 38, 40
Oak Street #2, 6, 7
Sever Street #30, 36, 38, 41
West Street #39, 44, 47, 49, 53, 54
William Street #56, 60, 61, 62–64, 66, 74, 75, 79, 80, 81, 84, 85, 87, 91, 93, 96, 98

OXFORD-CROWN DISTRICT

The Oxford-Crown District is made up of two contiguous areas:
    1) the Oxford-Crown Historic District, and
    2) the Oxford-Crown Extension District.

1) The Historic District covers approximately 7.5 acres containing 29 structures near the center of downtown Worcester. It is significant not only as a section of the city distinguished by the greatest concentration of Greek Revival houses, but also as historical evidence of an important period of Worcester's growth. With the exception of the Oxford Street School, the former Friends Meeting House, and the Pleasant Street Baptist Church, the buildings are residential. This section grew during the 1840s and 1850s as Worcester expanded during its transformation from a small agricultural and shire town into a large industrial city.

The District was once part of a tract of land owned by Major Daniel Ward. It extended from Main Street almost to Newbury Street, and from Pleasant Street nearly to Austin Street. Major Ward built his house to the north of the present Barton Place about 1720, lived there for 30 years, then sold the property to Sheriff Gardner Chandler for 326 pounds. Sheriff Chandler erected his mansion on the property at the corner of Main Street and Barton Place. Later, the property was sold to John Bush.

In 1818 this 30-acre tract was purchased for $9,000 by Benjamin Butman from Bush and his sons, Jonas and Richard. With the idea of developing the property, Butman had it surveyed by R. H. Eddy, a Boston engineer. In 1836 Eddy prepared a subdivision plan.

The section was to be known as "Park Hill." Butman envisioned a spacious residential area (with unusually large lots and a small central, ornamental park) because the lots shown on Eddy's plan were all unusually large for town or city lots, 80' x 150', or a total of 12,000 square feet. A number of these were sold for prices ranging from $85.00 for a lot in the middle of High Street to $260 for two lots sold to Isaac Davis between Park (now Oxford) and Crown Streets facing the park. Only two lots were sold on Park Street and none on Crown Street.

When Butman's business failed following the panic of 1837, his various real estate holdings scattered about Worcester fell into other hands. "Park Hill" appears to have been broken up into numerous parcels, with Isaac Davis taking over the largest part.

At this time the original subdivision plan was abandoned. All the lots were reduced in size, probably resulting in greater profits for the developer than under Butman's plan. The land originally designated park land was sold off in separate lots of various sizes. The smaller lots and the lack of a master plan changed the character of the area from the proposed elegant, planned, residential area to a neighborhood of smaller, simpler homes owned by small businessmen and craftsmen, and built by local carpenter-builders. These simple, well-balanced Greek Revival houses are modest, middle class counterparts of the larger, more imposing houses (such as the Salisbury House and the Taylor-Dowley Mansion) built in Worcester about the same time.

Today the Oxford-Crown neighborhood remains much as it was in the 19th century. The houses themselves are relatively unspoiled by additions, subtractions, or modern artificial siding. The area is still residential with most of the homes

Pleasant Street Baptist Church
130-O

2 Congress Street
130-O

owner-occupied. Because there are few buildings in the area built later than 1860, and because there is no encroachment by commercial and industrial building, the Oxford-Crown Historic District still has the quality of the era in which it was built.

2) The Extension District includes properties on Ashland, Austin, Chatham, Congress, Crown and Pleasant Streets which contain buildings of the same period and quality of the Historic District. Although some demolitions have taken place, the majority of buildings built prior to 1870 remain. Most are of the popular side-hall floor plan with gabled facade. Many are pure Greek Revival in style, while others (such as 95 and 103 Austin Street, ca. 1851–1860) combine elements of Greek Revival architecture with brackets and open porch supports more characteristic of Italianate Victorian. In addition, the area contains several rare building types. Among these: 98 Austin Street (ca. 1851), one of Worcester's few temple front Greek Revival style houses; 21 Crown Street (ca. 1851–1860), a double house of brick combining elements of Greek Revival and Italianate with heavy brackets; 1 Congress Street (ca. 1851–1860), the porch of which has four columns with combination Corinthian/Lotus capitals. Streets in this area were opened about the same time as those in the Historic District, and were settled by artisans, small-scale businessmen, and manufacturers.

Ashland Street #1-7
Austin Street #95, 98, 99, 101, 102, 103, 104, 107, 109, 110, 113, 114
Chatham Street #58-60, 66-68, 77, 78
Congress Street #1, 2, 4, 5, 6, 7, 8-10, 12, 13, 14, 15, 16
Crown Street #1, 3, 4, 5, 6, 7, 8-10, 9, 11, 12, 14, 16, 18, 19, 21-23, 24, 28
Oxford Street #7, 9, 10, 11, 14, 15, 18, 19, 23, 26
Oxford Place #1, 2, 3
Pleasant Street #144, 150, 167, 179, 187, 195

MAY STREET DISTRICT

Located at the crest of a ridge, the May Street District preserves a dense cluster of Queen Anne style houses as well as several earlier Victorian houses which pre-date the district's major development between 1888 and 1893. Although May Street existed prior to 1833, few buildings were built on it prior to 1851 when only two houses stood east of the May Street district boundaries. By 1860, the fashionable development of Main Street South led to the construction of several more houses at the east end of May Street, including the country estate of Benjamin Butman (now demolished). A subdivision extended along the north side of May Street and northward between modern Dewey and Hollywood Streets. Although this subdivision remained largely undeveloped until the 1880s, it established lot lines and the street pattern which remain today. Gradually, properties on the south side of May Street were subdivided during the 1870s, although house building continued to be restricted to the street's eastern end near Main Street.

The first house to be built within the May Street District was the B. D. Allen House of 1867 (30 May Street). Standing at the district's eastern boundary, this house is a good example of Second Empire architecture, one which retains its original entry porch, decorated window trim, dormers and brackets. Soon after the Allen House was built, Ebenezer Abbott (a real estate developer) built a large Second Empire style house at the corner of May and Woodland Streets (33 May Street—1873). Built, perhaps, to enhance the area's appeal to prospective buyers, this house retains most of its Second Empire style details on the first two storeys. In 1891, the Abbott House was enlarged by the addition of a full third storey, plus tower and rear wing to allow its conversion to the "Home School" for girls. In the late 1870s and early 1880s, several Victorian Gothic style houses appeared of which 32 May Street (built for William Hill around 1878) is an outstanding example in unaltered condition.

Between 1888 and 1893, all remaining lots in the district were built up with large Queen Anne style houses most of which appear to have been architect-designed. Of the houses built at this time, the John McGuire house is the most characteristically Queen Anne with a complex roof, gables, eyebrow dormers,

38 May Street
141-A-1

33-39 May Street
141-A-1

porches (first and second storeys) and varied sash. Although altered by asphalt shingles, the McGuire House retains all the essential features of its original design. Other notable examples of Queen Anne architecture are 39 and 40 May Street (both of which have corner towers) and 42 May Street (with ornate first and second storey porches). At present most buildings in the district are largely unaltered and present good examples of suburban architecture of the late nineteenth century.

May Street #29, 30, 31, 32, 33, 34, 35, 36, 37, 38, 39, 40, 41, 42, 43, 44, 46, 49, 51

CASTLE STREET ROW DISTRICT
4–18 Castle Street

Worcester's largest block of row houses, the Castle Street Row, contains eight units each of which is built of brick, two and one half storeys high, rising from a high basement. Each house has a side hall floor plan, three-sided bay window, bracketed entry porch and mansard roof with dormers. The lower four units of the row (4-10) are arranged symmetrically around two sets of paired entries, while the upper four units (12-18) have individual entries arranged at staggered heights which reflect the slope of the hill. With the exception of modern asphalt-shingle roofs and some modern pointing, the row retains most of its original simple features.

The site of the Castle Street Row was part of a much larger tract of land on which Eli Thayer had founded the Oread Institute, a women's college, in 1849. Built at the head of Castle Street, the Oread Institute was a large Gothic Revival building with corner towers and crenellations. Its castle-like appearance influenced the naming of surrounding streets. In the early 1870s, Thayer subdivided a portion of the Oread campus and sold off building lots to help liquidate a $20,000 mortgage on the property. Thayer apparently set the circumstances for a dense row house district by creating small narrow lots, virtually all of which were purchased by Larkin Gates, a local builder. Between 1868 and 1873, Gates built forty-two individual houses in the area, divided among eight Second Empire style rows. Of

Castle Street Row
141-D-1

these houses only the Castle Street row remains intact.

Although designed as modest, single-family homes, many of the houses of the Castle Street Row and neighboring rows were subdivided into apartments by the 1880s, while others contained a large number of boarders. Despite the apparent economy of the row-house type and despite Thayer's and Gate's efforts to establish it in the vicinity of Main Street South, row houses have been rare throughout Worcester's history. Castle Street contained the city's largest concentration.

Castle Street #4, 6, 8, 10, 12, 14, 16, 18

WELLINGTON STREET APARTMENT HOUSE DISTRICT

The Wellington Street Apartment House District includes properties on Wellington Street, Irving Street, and Jaques Avenue. It contains the densest sections remaining of a once extensive apartment house district which, until recent demolitions, covered an area from Main Street South to Chandler Street. One of the city's earliest centers of apartment construction, this larger area began to be developed in the mid-1880s.

Although Wellington Street contained one side hall plan Greek Revival style house (#62, demolished) built in 1851 for L. & S. P. Harrington, carpenters and real estate developers, it was virtually undeveloped prior to 1885 when Thomas J. Barrett, a mason, built his two storey brick, Queen Anne style house at #41. Soon after the completion of the Barrett House, a large number of owner-occupied, three and four storey apartment houses were constructed on Wellington Street and Jaques Avenue. Built of brick, these apartment houses shared the same floor plans as many of the city's "three-deckers," and were of smaller scale than buildings of the same period on Main Street. Decoration of these buildings is limited to rock-faced sandstone trim, arched entries, and decorative brickwork at the cornice.

Beginning with the construction of "the Columbia" (6 Jaques Avenue) in 1892, later apartment houses in the district were built on the scale of Main Street buildings and employed center entrance/central hall plans with at least two apartments per storey. Unlike the earlier set of buildings, these later apartment

49 Wellington Street
142-T-2

1, 5 Jaques Avenue
142-T-2

houses were owned, designed, and constructed by builder/developers, who maintained them as income properties. Architecturally they vary from the eclectic combination of brick, granite, and terra cotta used in the Columbia, to "the Knowlton" with its double bay windows and carved sandstone entry, and the more severe design of 42 Wellington Street which is nearly undecorated except for its fine sandstone basement and one and one half storey entry surround.

Also included in the district is the First Freewill Baptist Church, a brick and granite building of eclectic, Gothic design. Designed by George Adams of Lawrence, Massachusetts, this building is unaltered, retaining original slate work, stained glass and terra cotta tiles.

Jaques Avenue #1, 5, 6
Wellington Street #23, 25, 37, 41, 42, 45, 46, 49, 51, 62, 63
Irving Street #25, 27

WOODLAND STREET DISTRICT

118, 114 Woodland Street
153-A

The Woodland Street District contains a mixture of well-preserved Victorian houses and exhibits a pattern of development which characterized many of the Victorian residential neighborhoods around Main Street South. The first development of this section began in the late 1860s. Between 1868 and 1881 seven houses were built on the west side of the street, most of them constructed on double house lots. Although some development of the east side took place, few buildings on this side of the street pre-date 1890. Among the most architecturally interesting houses from this first period is the John Hill House, 140 Woodland. First occupied in 1876 by John Hill, owner of the National Manufacturing Company, this house has an unusual "L" floor plan with the main entry of the house located at the junction of the two wings and set at a 45 degree angle to both wings. Virtually unaltered, the Hill House retains gable aprons, decorated window caps, and a fine, original front porch. In addition, the Henry Farrar House, 110 Woodland Street (ca. 1877), and the Wade Hill House, 114 Woodland Street (1881), are good examples of local Victorian Gothic architecture, particularly the former which remains nearly unaltered. Also built in the street's first wave of development were a number of Second Empire style houses. The Henry Taft House, 118 Woodland Street (ca. 1868), although altered, is the best example.

By the 1890s, Woodland Street, which had been on the city's outer fringe in the 1860s and 1870s, was completely surrounded by residential neighborhoods. The pressure of increasing population and apparent rising land values led to the area's more dense redevelopment. Between Loudon and Hawthorne Streets, the "Slater Estate" was demolished and the land subdivided into smaller house lots. On the west side of Woodland Street, all the original double lots were subdivided and new houses constructed on what had been the side yards of earlier houses. Notable buildings from this period of development (ca. 1890-1905) include All Souls' Universalist Church, ca. 1891, a Queen Anne style wood frame church; 130 Woodland Street, a Queen Anne style house; and 138 Woodland Street, an ornate building of mixed Colonial Revival and Queen Anne style architecture. The Frank Heath House (ca. 1904), at the south corner of Woodland and Loudon Streets, is an especially fine example of Colonial Revival style, with a nearly square floor plan, a high hip roof, a porch across its facade, and another on its west wall. The house is richly decorated with Colonial Revival details, including Palladian windows framed by Ionic columns set out from the main body of the building. Many of the details of the Heath House are reminiscent of the William Inman House of 1897-1898 at 7 Oak Street which was designed by George Clemence.

Hawthorne Street #11, 12
Loudon Street #11, 24
Norwood Street #10
Woodland Street #104, 105, 106, 110, 114, 118, 124, 126, 130, 134, 138, 140, 143

11 Loudon Street
153-A

THREE-DECKERS

Because of the large numbers of three-deckers remaining in Worcester (still very much in use and most well cared for), no individual building or district was nominated for inclusion in the National Register during the first multiple listing survey of Worcester buildings in 1978.

Nonetheless, this building type has played such an important role in the city's development that some three-deckers should be recognized for their historic value. To this end, we expect recognition to be forthcoming in the near future.

"If God had intended man to work in Worcester and live in Marlboro, He would never have created the three-decker." This quote from a 1970 article in the *Worcester Telegram* was right on the mark. Three-decker creation was inevitable, for between 1880 and 1930 Worcester's population burgeoned from 60,000 to 195,000. To absorb that growth, the three-decker was "invented" and over 6,000 were built (4,000 of these in the thirty years between 1890 and 1920). As an adventure in family housing, it turned out to be an eminently practical answer to a serious problem.

The first three-decker was built ca. 1858 on Endicott or John Streets. Building records indicate that from 1890 to 1910 nearly one-half of all construction in Worcester consisted of three-deckers. In 1946, returning WWII veterans found that half the city's rental units were three-decker apartments. No new three-deckers have been built since 1936, but according to the 1980 census they still provide about one-fifth of the city's housing units.

Indigenous to New England, and a few Middle Atlantic states, these large, three storey buildings are still common sights in most mill and factory towns. Because Worcester spawned more than most, it became known as the "City of Three-Deckers." Solidly built of quality materials, with big, airy rooms and plenty of closets, they have provided excellent family housing for three-quarters of a century. Recent estimates place the number still remaining in Worcester at about 4500.

OBITUARIES

The following are structures in Worcester once listed in the National Register of Historic Places but torn down soon after. The year listed first is the year of construction; the year listed last is the year of demolition.

Emory Banister House
3 Harvard Street
Elbridge Boyden, architect
1847–1981

Charles Chamberlain House
372 Pleasant Street
1876–1984

Tyler Curtis House
548 Lincoln Street
1848–1978

Foster Block
404–406 Main Street
Elbridge Boyden, architect
1854–1972

Goddard House
12 Catharine Street
Elbridge Boyden, architect
1870–1979

Levi Lincoln Block
201–205 Main Street
1818–1979

E. T. Smith House (Post #479 VFW)
839 Main Street
1889–1982

Worcester Consolidated Street
   Railway Company
99–109 Main Street
Lucius W. Briggs, architect
ca. 1903–1980

EARLY WORCESTER ARCHITECTS

Beginning with the arrival of Elias Carter, master-builder/architect, in 1828, Worcester developed a strong tradition of employing local architects to design private homes. Although knowledge of Carter's work is limited to the mansions he designed for Worcester's established upper class, later architects were increasingly employed by the rising class of manufacturers which emerged in the 1840s and 1850s. By 1850, six architects are known to have had offices in Worcester and, by 1875, an additional thirteen had been listed in local directories. Between the time of Carter's arrival and 1900, at least fifty-five architects are known to have worked in the city.

Although large numbers of architects were available, several firms and individuals dominated the profession locally. Among the most successful were Elbridge Boyden (1847-1898); Amos P. Cutting (1867-1896); Stephen C. Earle (1867-1913), a member of the firm of Earle & Fuller (1867-1876), later Earle & Fisher (1892-1903) which also maintained a Boston office in the late 1870s; Fuller & Delano (1879-1901)—Fuller was formerly a partner of Stephen Earle; Barker & Nourse (1880-1902); George H. Clemence (1893-1924); and Lucius W. Briggs (1896-1940), member of the firm of Frost, Briggs & Chamberlain (1900-1912). To a surprising degree, local histories, city business directories, and illustrated guides of nineteenth century Worcester name the architects both of prominent public buildings and of some of the city's more elaborate houses. In addition, the number of nineteenth century architects whose work was already known prior to this survey suggests that the profession was highly respected locally.

The rapid, continuous growth of Worcester, sparked by a boom in the late 1840s, resulted in the construction of large numbers of single-family houses in the various Victorian styles which rose and fell in popularity between 1850 and 1900. Of these styles, the Greek Revival is represented by several grand houses designed by Elias Carter or designed in his manner, and by a number of simple, side-hall plan houses with pedimented gables and Doric porches. Nineteenth century photographs and local illustrated guide books show that a particularly large number of opulent Italianate style houses were built during the 1850s. Many of these were high-style houses of stone or brick construction covered in mastic and identified as the work of Elbridge Boyden in his obituaries. Of all the Victorian styles found locally, the Italianate has become the rarest, both through alteration and demolition, although a few examples remain which may be able to be restored. Beginning with the Second Empire style which became popular in Worcester in the late 1850s, Worcester has good examples of the various Victorian house styles located mainly in the central section of the city.

GLOSSARY OF TERMS

acanthus—an ornamentation representing leaves of prickly herbs.

acroteria—pedestals for sculpture or ornament at each base or apex of a pediment.

arabesque—ornament or style using flower, fruit, and sometimes animal outlines to produce a pattern.

architrave—the molding around a door or other rectangular opening.

ashlar—building stone which has been squared and dressed.

barge board—decorative board attached to projecting portion of a gable roof.

bracket—a supporting member projecting from the face of a wall.

capital—moldings or carvings forming a finish to the top of a column.

cartouche—an ornate or ornamental frame.

chamfer—a beveled edge.

coffered—referring to a recessed panel in a ceiling.

console—architectural member of projection from a wall to form a bracket.

coping—the covering course of a wall.

corbel—strong supporting member built into but projecting from a wall to carry a heavy load such as roof truss; similar to a bracket but stronger.

Corinthian—the lightest and most ornate of the three Greek orders of architecture characterized by its bell-shaped capital covered with acanthus.

cornice—a top course that crowns a wall.

corona—the projecting part of a classic cornice.

cresting—culminating in an upper prominence, edge or limit.

crocket—an ornament usually in the form of curved and bent foliage used on the edge of a gable or spire.

dentil—one of a series of small projecting rectangular blocks especially under a cornice.

distyle—having two columns on one or either front.

diapering—to ornament with a pattern consisting of small repeated units of design connecting with one another.

Doric—the oldest and simplest of the classical Greek orders characterized by heavy fluted columns with no base and plain saucer-shaped capitals.

dormer—the roofed structure containing a window.

eclectic—selecting what appears to be best in various designs; composed of elements drawn from various sources.

entablature—upper section of a wall or storey that usually is supported on columns or pilasters; in classical orders consists of architrave, frieze, and cornice.

facade—the front of a building usually given special treatment.

fenestration—arrangement, proportioning, and design of windows and doors in a building.

foliate—shaped like a leaf or composed of leaves.

fret—an ornamental network.

frieze—a sculptured or richly ornamented band; the part of an entablature between architrave and cornice.

gable—the vertical triangular end of a building from eaves to ridge; the end wall of a building.

guilloche—an architectural ornament formed of interlaced bands with openings containing round devices.

hipped roof—a roof which pitches inward from all four sides.

incise—to carve figures, letters or devices into.

Ionic—the Greek order of architecture characterized by the spiral volutes of its capital.

keystone—the wedge-shaped piece at the crown of an arch that locks other pieces in place.

lintel—a horizontal member spanning and usually carrying a load above an opening.

lunette—that surface at the upper part of a wall which is partly surrounded by a vault which the wall intersects.

mansard—a roof having two slopes on all sides with the lower slope steeper than the upper.

medallion—a tablet or panel in a wall or window bearing a figure in relief, a portrait, or an ornament.

modillion—an ornamental block or bracket under a corona of the cornice in the Corinthian and other orders.

mortise—a rectangular cavity cut into a piece of material to receive a tenon.

muntin—a strip separating panes of glass in a sash.

oculus—a circular opening in a ceiling or wall.

ogee—a molding with an S-shaped profile or a pointed arch having on each side a reversed curve near the apex.

oriel—a large bay window projecting from a wall and supported by a corbel or bracket.

Palladian—relating to a revived classic style in architecture based on the works of Andrea Palladio.

paterae—an embossed ornament in the shape of a circle.

pavilion—a part of a building projecting from the rest.

pediment—a triangular space forming the gable of a 2-pitched roof in classic architecture.

peripteral—surrounded by a single row of columns.

piano mobile—when longer windows are on upper floor marking the family's living area.

pilaster—the projecting part of a square column which is attached to a wall; it is finished with the same cap and base as a free-standing column.

plinth—a square block serving as a base; the lowest member of a base.

porte cochère—a passageway through a building designed to let vehicles pass from street to courtyard.

quatrefoil—a conventionalized representation of a flower with four petals or of a leaf with four leaflets.

quoin—one of the blocks forming the solid exterior angle of a building.

rusticate—to bevel or rebate (as the edges of stone blocks) to make the joints conspicuous.

scroll—a spiral or convoluted form in ornamental design.

sill—a horizontal piece that forms the lowest member of a framework or supporting structure.

springer—a stone or other solid laid at the impost of an arch.

soffit—the underside of a part of a building.

surrounds—a border or edging that surrounds.

swag—something hanging in a curve between two points.

tenon—a projecting member in a piece of material for insertion into a mortise to make a joint.

terra cotta—a glazed or unglazed fired clay used for statuettes, vases and architectural purposes (as roofing, facing, and relief ornamentation).

trabeated—designed or constructed of horizontal beams or lintels.

trefoil—an ornament or symbol in the form of a stylized trifoliate.

triglyph—a slightly projecting rectangular tablet in a Doric frieze with two vertical channels of V section and two corresponding chamfers of half channels on the vertical sides.

volute—a spiral or scroll-shaped form; a spiral scroll-shaped ornament forming the chief feature of the Ionic capital.

voussoir—one of the wedge-shaped pieces forming an arch or vault.

BIBLIOGRAPHY

Major Sources

Maps & Atlases

1828   *Map of Worcester.* Worcester: Worcester Village Register, 1828.

1833   Stebbins, H. *Map of Worcester, Shire Town of the County of Worcester.* Boston: C. Harris, 1833.

1851   Walling, H. *Map of the City of Worcester.* (2 rolls). (Boston?): Warren Lazell, 1851.

c. 1860   Ball, P. *Map of the City of Worcester, Massachusetts.* (Worcester?): Smith & McKinney, undated.

1870   Beers, F. W. *Atlas of the City of Worcester, Massachusetts.* New York: F. W. Beers & Co., 1870.

1877   Wall, Caleb & Triscott, S. *Map of Worcester, Massachusetts—Showing Oldest Roads and Location of Earliest Settlers.* Worcester: Tyler & Seagrave, 1877. (Printed in conjunction with Caleb Wall's *Reminiscences of Worcester.*)

1878   Triscott, S. P. R. *Map of the City of Worcester.* Boston: G. H. Walker, 1878.

1886 Hopkins, G. M. *Atlas of the City of Worcester, Massachusetts.* Philadelphia: G. M. Hopkins, 1886.

1896   Richards, L. J. & Co. *Atlas of the City of Worcester, Massachusetts.* Springfield: L. J. Richards & Co., 1896.

1911   Richards, L. J. & Co. *Atlas of the City of Worcester, Massachusetts.* Springfield: L. J. Richards & Co., 1911.

1922   Richards, L. J. & Co. *Atlas of the City of Worcester, Massachusetts.* Springfield: Richards Map Co., 1922.

1936   Sanborn Map Co. *Insurance Maps of Worcester, Massachusetts* (4 vol.). New York: Sanborn Map Co., 1936.

Photographic Collections

Worcester Historical Museum, Worcester, Massachusetts.

Unpublished Sources

Waite, Albert G. Notes pertaining to residential structures which existed on selected streets in the City of Worcester, Massachusetts. Unpublished manuscript in possession of the American Antiquarian Society, Worcester, Massachusetts.

Worcester County Registry of Deeds, Worcester, Massachusetts. (Plan & Record Books as cited on individual forms.)

Periodicals

American Architect and Building News. (cited on individual forms.)

The Builders' Weekly. Worcester: the Builders' Weekly Co., 10/2/1897 (Vol. I, no. 1)—ca. 1900.

Engineering Record. title varies: *The Plumber & Sanitary Engineer,* Vol. I-III; *The Sanitary Engineer,* Vol. IV-XVI; *The Engineering & Building Record,* Vol. XVII-XXI; *Engineering Record,* Vol. XXII-present.

The Practical Mechanic. Worcester: F. S. Blanchard Co., 7/1887 (Vol. I, no. 1)—ca. 1892.

The Worcester Commercial and Board of Trade. Worcester: F. S. Blanchard Co., 5/1892 (Vol. I, no. 1)—3/1893 (?).

The Worcester County Weekly Record. Worcester: New England Record & Reporting Co., 1903-1915.

The Worcester Magazine. Worcester: Board of Trade & Chamber of Commerce, 1/1901 (Vol. I, no. 1)—6/19/16.

Secondary Sources

Ambler, James Arthur. *Worcester Illustrated.* Worcester: J. A. Ambler & Co., 1875.

Baker, Zephaniah. *Cottage Builders Manual.* Worcester: Z. Baker & Co., 1856.

Crane, Ellery Bicknell. *Historic Homes and Institutions and Genealogical and Personal Memoirs of Worcester County, Massachusetts.* (4 vol.) New York: Lewis Publishing Co., 1907.

Cummings, C. H. *Leading Businessmen of Worcester and Vicinity.* Boston: Mercantile Publishing Co., 1889.

Howland, H. J. *Worcester in 1850.* Worcester: H. J. Howland, 1850.

Howland, H. J. *The Heart of the Commonwealth.* Worcester: H. J. Howland, 1856 (reprinted, 1861).

Hyde, A. W. *Worcester, Its Past and Present.* Worcester: Oliver B. Wood, 1888.

Kingsley, E. & Knab, F. *Picturesque Worcester* (3 vol.). Springfield: W. F. Adams Co., 1895.

Lincoln, W. *History of Worcester.* Worcester: Moses D. Phillips & Co., 1837.

Lincoln, W. & Hersey, C. *History of Worcester.* Worcester: pub. by Charles Hersey, printed by Henry J. Howland, 1862.

Nelson, John. *Worcester County: A Narrative History* (3 vol.). New York: American Historical Society, Inc., 1934.

Nutt, Charles. *History of Worcester and Its People* (4 vol.). New York: Lewis Historical Publishing Co., 1919.

Rice, F. P. *Dictionary of Worcester and Its Vicinity.* Worcester: F. P. Rice, 1893.

Rice, F. P. (ed.). *The Worcester of 1898, Fifty Years a City.* Worcester: F. S. Blanchard & Co., 1899.

Rice, F. P. *Worcester Vital Statistics to 1848.* Worcester: Worcester Historical Society, 1894.

Wall, Caleb A. *Reminiscences of Worcester.* Worcester: Tyler & Seagrave, 1877.

Washburn, Charles G. *Industrial Worcester.* Worcester: The Davis Press, 1917.

Worcester Board of Trade. *A Tribute to the Columbian Year.* Worcester: F. S. Blanchard & Co., 1893.

_____, *Art Work of Worcester* (12 parts). Chicago: W. H. Parish Publishing Co., 1894.

_____, *City of Worcester, Its Public Buildings and Businesses.* Worcester: Sanford & Davis, 1886.

_____, *Worcester City Documents,* printed annually, series begins with #1 for the year ending 3/31/1849.

_____, *History of Worcester County, Massachusetts* (2 vol.). Boston: C. F. Jewett & Co., 1879.

_____, *Illustrated Business Guide of the City of Worcester, Massachusetts.* Worcester: Snow, Woodman & Co., 1881.

Worcester Almanac Directory and Business Advertiser (title becomes *Worcester Directory* after 1858). Worcester: publisher varies, annually 1844 to present.

Worcester House Directory. Worcester: publisher varies, bi-annually 1888 to present.

Worcester Town Records. 1722-1848.

Worcester Village Register. Worcester: 1828.

Index of Buildings by Street

Index of Buildings by Style

Index by Builder

The symbol in the cover design is taken from the seal of the Worcester Heritage Preservation Society and is the Brand Mark of Worcester, designated by the General Court in 1684. The dates around the seal represent the first, second and final settlements of Worcester.

Design by Marian L. Bates

Typesetting and printing by Commonwealth Press, Worcester, Massachusetts

Type: Hanover
Cover: Lustro Offset Enamel Dull 100#
Text: Lustro Offset Enamel Dull 80#
*   S. D. Warren Company*
*   A Division of Scott Paper Company*